Learning through Literature

Fun Language Arts Activities with a Math Twist

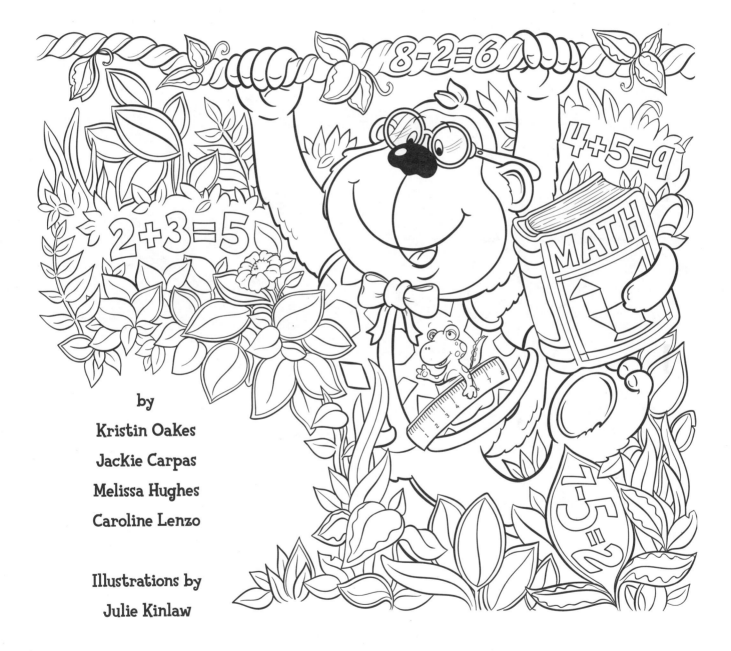

by

Kristin Oakes

Jackie Carpas

Melissa Hughes

Caroline Lenzo

Illustrations by

Julie Kinlaw

Carson-Dellosa Publishing, Inc.

Greensboro, North Carolina

Credits

Editors: Louise Vaughn, Karen Seberg, Debra Olson Pressnall
Cover and inside illustrations: Julie Kinlaw
Cover design and production: Annette Hollister-Papp
Page production: Louise Vaughn, Mark Conrad

ISBN 0-88724-259-6

Table of Contents

One fish, two fish
Red fish, blue fish.
Dr. Seuss, 1960

Rather than dividing class instruction into separate subject areas, there has been an increasing trend to present topics and concepts in an integrated approach. Educators are finding creative, effective methods to design interdisciplinary learning experiences which help students make relevant connections between new and prior knowledge. Teachers know that children's literature can bring content area studies to life. Rich literature can become the lens through which students learn new ideas, processes, and skills.

Learning through Literature is designed to provide teachers with ideas and activities that will enhance mathematics instruction. Research has shown that students comprehend and retain new concepts much better when the material has meaning or authentic application for them. Literature can nurture genuine curiosity about real-world experiences and foster the desire to discover through the use of intriguing stories, fascinating illustrations, and interesting characters. Math-related literature is a great tool to stimulate inquiry and support the critical-thinking, application, and problem-solving skills of mathematics. Through this inquiry-based approach to learning, students accept an "invitation" to learn and move to the center of an active learning process. They are able to see mathematical concepts in more relative terms, ask meaningful questions about them, and construct a conceptual framework for application.

Each unit in this book includes cross-curricular activities that will reinforce concepts and strengthen skills as well as make mathematics instruction much more personal for students. Concept maps are included to illustrate the cross-curricular activities, author ideas for writing experiences, and at-home activities that support an area of mathematics instruction. Introductory lessons, reinforcement strategies, and culminating activities are included to help teachers use rich literature to assess prior knowledge, spark interest, build authentic contexts for learning, and address multiple learning styles and intelligences. From number sense and math facts to measurement and money, this book can help classroom teachers use children's literature as a powerful complement to mathematics instruction.

Reading Strategies

Pre-reading strategies offer teachers a chance to "hook" their students on math topics. Before beginning an activity, introduce the literature selection by reading aloud the title and author of the book and showing the book's cover. Then ask your students to explain how they think the book applies to the current unit of study. These preliminary activities not only prepare students for the lesson, but they also begin to build understanding of the mathematics principles the literature addresses.

Guided reading strategies provide opportunities to reinforce mathematical concepts, stimulate further inquiry, and link formal mathematics concepts to real-world problems and contexts. These class discussions can act as a springboard for hands-on math explorations. During the lessons, you can use the literature selections to explain *why* certain skills are used, while establishing a strong connection with *how* the process is completed.

Post-reading strategies encourage students to explore new math ideas and raise questions as they synthesize information. This resource book contains a variety of language arts activities that enable students to reflect on their learning and respond critically. Art, music, and drama activities can also be effective ways to allow kinesthetic learners to demonstrate their understanding of math concepts. The culminating activities address multiple learning styles and foster creative expression as alternatives to traditional mathematics practice and assessment.

Assessments

As teachers, we all want our students to enjoy learning. Creating art projects, role-playing stories, and writing poetry about math concepts can all be fun for students. By providing students a variety of opportunities to demonstrate their learning, teachers are also accommodating individual learning styles and intelligences. However, some educators find it difficult to assess student learning in these kinds of activities and provide a measurement in the form of a grade. Included in this book are assessment tools and evaluation strategies that can apply to all of the activities and explorations. The important thing to remember with any assessment tool is to focus on the objective of the lesson, that is, what it is you want your students to learn from engaging in a specific activity. Once you have clearly identified the objective, then you need to determine how the students will be able to demonstrate these skills or knowledge through the activity. For example, if you have chosen to engage your students in an art activity from this book, there are several ways to assess their learning. You could create a simple checklist as shown below that you can use informally with each child.

Project: Pattern Pictures (shapes and patterns)	
Student:	**Date:**
☐ The student has successfully created a pattern on each side of the border.	
☐ The student has accurately identified the pattern in the picture.	
☐ The student is able to describe the pattern that he/she has created.	

Some math activities involve the use of manipulatives to teach a specific skill. These activities can also be assessed by completing a chart to document each student's progress. This kind of informal assessment data is often useful when conferencing with parents. Certainly, it isn't necessary to grade your students' work for every activity, especially introductory or practice assignments. One way to document each student's progress, even in large group instruction, is simply to write the students'

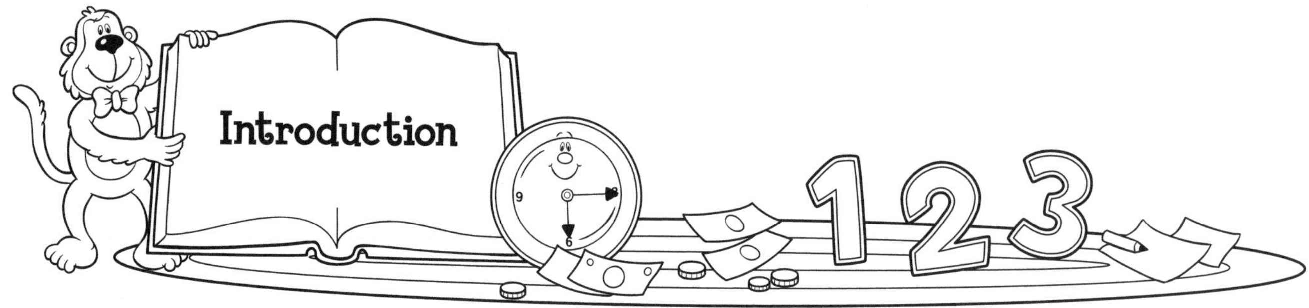

names on the lines of a chart and note the skill being assessed at the top of each column. When the student demonstrates mastery of a skill, check the appropriate column. You may even want to use a check minus or check plus system. Keep this sheet handy on a clipboard so that you can update the chart each time a skill is introduced or practiced.

Project assessment charts can also be used to evaluate a variety of tasks across the curriculum. The open grading chart (see page 8 for reproducible chart) can be modified to measure student learning in the form of pupil performance outcomes or learning goals. To complete the chart, fill in the first column with the goals or objectives of the activity. Share the grading criteria with students as you introduce the assignment to define your expectations clearly. You could also create the grading criteria together as a class. In this way, students are informed about the objectives of the project and actively involved in establishing high standards for quality work. Make sure you keep the goals clear and concise and use language students can understand.

Project:			
Student:	Date:		
Objectives	Great Job!	Good!	Keep Working!
1.	3	2	1
2.	3	2	1
3.	3	2	1
4.	3	2	1
Total Points:			

Name:____________________ Date:________

Color the face to show how you would rate your work on the ________________ project.

This is my best work.

I can do better next time.

This was not my best effort!

Other examples of project assessment charts are also provided. Self-evaluation of a project (see pages 7 and 8 for reproducible student evaluation forms) is an effective tool for young students to use to reflect on their own work. Even very young students can use this form to monitor their own progress on projects and evaluate areas of weakness.

Parent Communication

Communicating clear expectations to parents is especially important at the primary level. Many parents want to be involved in their children's education, but do not know how to help. A simple letter communicating upcoming units of study can be a remarkably effective way to keep parents involved and interested in what students are learning at school. At-home activities give parents opportunities to reinforce math concepts being taught and share rich literature with their children. Each unit in this book contains sample parent letters and at-home activities that will encourage parental involvement and support.

Student Evaluation Form for (project) ______________________________

Name: ______________________________	pleased	disappointed
This is how I feel about my finished project:	☺	☹
This is how I feel about how hard I worked on my project:	☺	☹
I think others will feel this way when they look at my work:	☺	☹
I feel this way when I think about doing another project:	☺	☹

Name: ______________________________ Date: ____________

Student Evaluation for ______________________________

I like my work because ______________________________

____

____

Next time I want to improve ______________________________

____

____

On a scale from 1 to 10, I would rate my effort on this project:

low 1 2 3 4 5 6 7 8 9 10 **high**

Student Evaluation Form / Open Grading Chart

Name:______________________________ Date:____________

Color the face to show how you would rate your work on the ____________________ project.

This is my best work.

I can do better next time.

This was not my best effort!

Project:

Student: Date:

Objectives	Great Job!	Good!	Keep Working!
1.	3	2	1
2.	3	2	1
3.	3	2	1
4.	3	2	1
Total Points:			

Counting 1... 2... 3... 4... 5... 6... 7... 8... 9... 10

Counting skills are the basis for good math skills, and these activities across the curriculum can help your students get plenty of practice in counting.

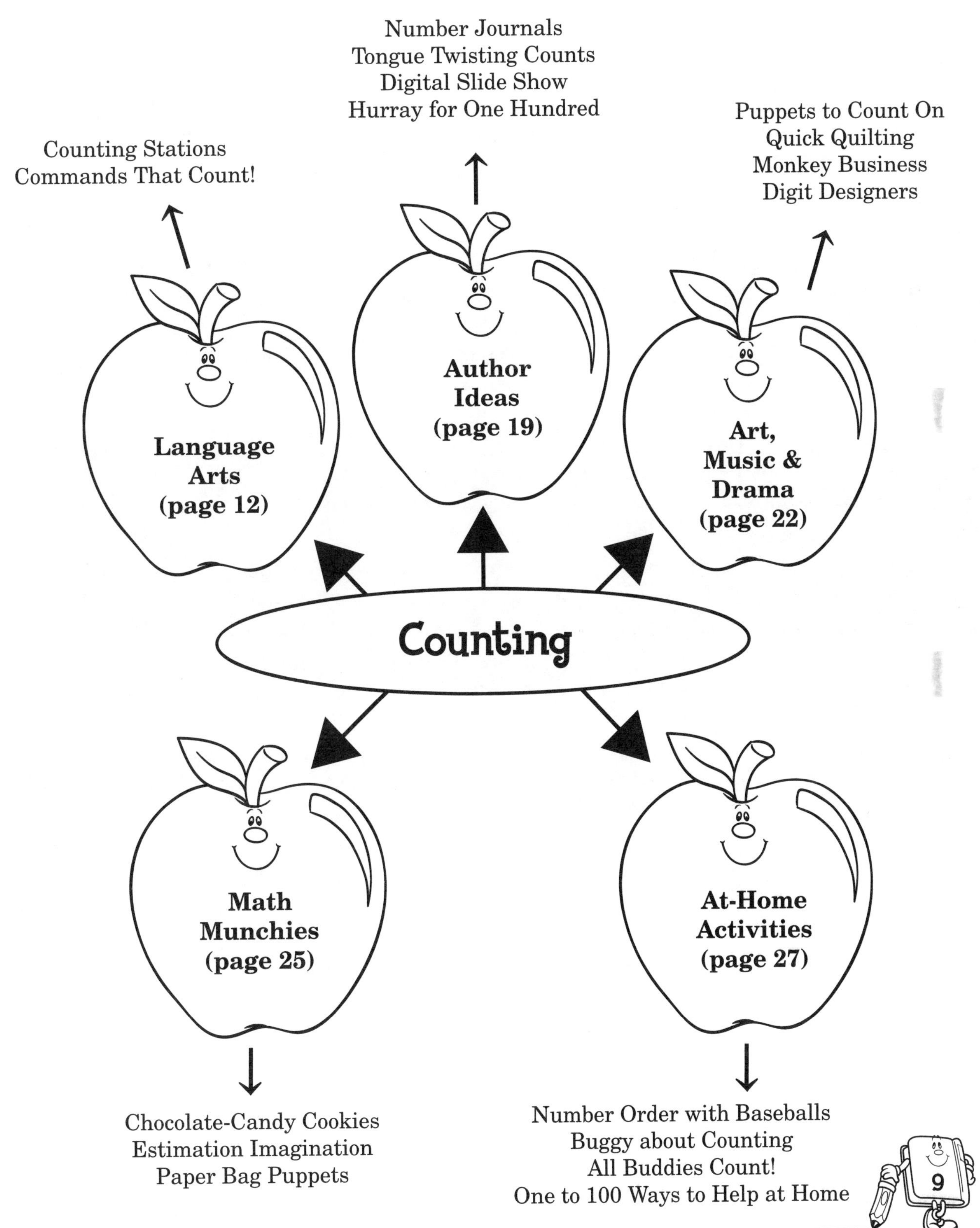

Featured Literature

The following selections are used in conjunction with the activities in this section. You may want to obtain them from your library before you start the unit. (Activities with which the books are used are listed in parentheses.)

100 Days of School, by Trudy Harris (Milbrook Press, 1999). Celebrate 100 days with this book of riddles. Readers will soon discover that each answer equals 100. (Hurray for One Hundred, page 21)

100 School Days, by Anne Rockwell (HarperCollins Publishers, 2002). This story follows a classroom through a school year as students put a penny in a jar for each day of school. (Hurray for One Hundred, page 21)

Arlene Alda's 1 2 3, by Arlene Alda (Tricycle Press, 1998). Stunning photography shows the numerals 1–10 and back again in nature. A two is found in a twisting kite string and a swan's neck reflected in the lake makes a three. (Digital Slide Show, page 20)

The Baseball Counting Book, by Barbara Barbieri McGrath (Charlesbridge Publishing, 1999). Students will have a ball counting with this baseball-themed book. From a beginning score of zero to twenty baseball cards, each page is a baseball fan's delight. Rhyming text and a glossary of baseball terms are included. (Number Order with Baseballs, page 27)

Count! by Denise Fleming (H. Holt, 1992). Colorful abstract art and unique animals are used in this simple counting book with few words. (Commands That Count! page 12)

Each Orange Had 8 Slices: A Counting Book, by Paul Giganti, Jr. (Greenwillow Books, 1992). Bright illustrations and simple text ask "How many?" on each page. Younger students can do straightforward counting, but older children can skip count and multiply to find the answers. (Counting Stations, page 12)

Every Buddy Counts, by Stuart J. Murphy (HarperCollins Publishers, 1997). A sad little girl becomes happy when she realizes just how many friends she has. She counts all of her buddies in the neighborhood, from one hamster and five next-door neighbors to ten teddy bears. (All Buddies Count! page 29)

Five Little Monkeys Jumping on the Bed, retold and illustrated by Eileen Christelow (Clarion Books, 1989). Five little monkeys jump on the bed until they all fall off and their mother puts them to bed. (Monkey Business, page 23)

How Many, How Many, How Many, by Rick Walton (Candlewick Press, 1993). Readers practice counting from one to twelve while answering simple questions about nursery rhymes, sports, and more (e.g., how many seasons in a year, how many fingers on one hand, and how many bears found Goldilocks sleeping). (Number Journals, page 19)

Let's Count, by Tana Hoban (Greenwillow Books, 1999). This book presents photographs of things found in a neighborhood that equal the numbers one through fifteen, and by tens to 100. Large numerals, the numbers in words, and dots are also shown on each page. (Digital Slide Show, page 20)

The M&M's Brand Counting Book, by Barbara Barbieri McGrath (Charlesbridge, 2002). McGrath uses M&M's® brand candies to explore counting from 1–12, sorting, and colors in this book. Illustrations feature the M&M's® characters and show each number in picture form, word, and numeral. (Chocolate-Candy Cookies, page 25)

My Little Sister Ate One Hare, by Bill Grossman (Crown Publishers, 1996). In this cumulative counting story, the narrator's sister keeps eating and eating. It is a funny new twist on the lovable Old Lady tale. (Paper Bag Puppets, page 26)

One Duck Stuck, by Phyllis Root (Candlewick Press, 1998). A duck becomes stuck in a marsh and groups of animals try to release him. Your students will love counting to ten as they eagerly await the ending. (Puppets to Count On, page 22)

One Hundred Hungry Ants, by Elinor J. Pinczes (Houghton Mifflin, 1993). One hundred ants march single file, then divide into two rows of 50, four rows of 20, etc., to get to a picnic. (One to 100 Ways to Help at Home, page 29)

One Moose, Twenty Mice, by Clare Beaton (Barefoot Books, Inc., 1999). Felt illustrations and hidden pictures are used in this simple counting book. Students can recognize and count numbers from one to twenty in this charming book. (Quick Quilting, page 23)

Ten Little Ladybugs, by Melanie Gerth (Piggy Toes Press, 2000). Readers are able to count backward from ten as the round plastic ladybugs fly away. The rhyming text also provides clues as to how many ladybugs are left. (Buggy about Counting, page 28)

Way Out in the Desert, by T. J. Marsh and Jennifer Ward (Rising Moon, 1998). A variation of the traditional "Over in the Meadow," featuring desert animals, this book has a numeral hidden in each illustration. (Digit Designers, page 24)

Additional Suggested Literature

10 in the Bed, by Anne Geddes (Photogenic Publishers, 2000). In this beautifully photographed book of babies, readers count from one to ten and back again. The story is told on a blanket in the middle of each page. It is unique because when you reach ten, the book can be turned over and read back to front!

Just Enough Carrots, by Stuart J. Murphy (HarperCollins Publishers, 1997). Murphy uses colorful illustrations to explore the concept of comparing amounts with the terms more, fewer, and the same.

Underwater Counting: Even Numbers, by Jerry Pallotta (Charlesbridge, 2001). This colorful book takes readers on a counting tour of the ocean with the numbers 0 to 50 by twos. The author provides factual information about the ocean animals included and the illustrator has hidden the numeral in each picture.

Counting Stations

Literature: *Each Orange Had 8 Slices: A Counting Book*, by Paul Giganti, Jr.

Materials: Paper, pencils, construction paper, patterns from pages 13–18, crayons, scissors, glue

Activity: Read the book *Each Orange Had 8 Slices*, by Paul Giganti, Jr., to your class and allow them time to count the answers on each page. This will be an exciting challenge since on some of the pages the reader must count as high as 45. Just reading and solving the book may take several sittings, but the time spent is well worth the effort considering all the counting practice your mathematicians will receive! Follow up this multifaceted story with some counting of your own at station time.

The materials needed for the station are a teacher-created instruction sheet, construction paper, crayons, scissors, and glue. You may want to have parent volunteers or older students use the patterns (pages 14, 16, and 18) and cut out the necessary pieces to shorten work time for the students. Each group of students will use the instruction sheet to construct a banana split, pizza, or salad. Use number words and rebus pictures in your instructions so even nonreaders can "read" and follow them. Adding a picture clue after each direction as well as showing a completed project will enable your students to work independently.

At the end of just one week of station time, you will have enough new materials to use in three different stations! Use one group of projects at a time and decorate a bulletin board close to the learning center. Once all the banana splits are displayed, for example, you can add a list of math questions much like the ones in *Each Orange Has 8 Slices*. How many ice cream scoops are there altogether? How many chocolate sprinkles are there? Students can write their answers in their journals, which can be kept in a basket at the center. The following week they can count pizza parts, and finally, the salad ingredients.

Commands That Count!

Literature: *Count!* by Denise Fleming

Materials: Paper, pencils, crayons

Activity: *Count!* is a colorful picture book written in commands that tell a number of animals to do just one action. Of course, the numbers increase as the students read through the book. Review sentence punctuation by incorporating counting with commands and exclamations. Give students an opportunity to read the text in this picture book as well as write their own simple commands. To add a challenge, teach students that action words are called verbs. Ask them to be sure that each command includes an action word or verb. Verbs can be written in red while exclamation marks can be shown in blue. Then number words can be traced in another color for a colorful display of commands that count!

Extension: Encourage your students to identify each sentence type (e.g., exclamatory, interrogative, imperative, statement) and write an example of each.

Here's the Scoop!
Glue items to the bowl in order:
• 1 yellow banana
• 3 of ice cream
• 1 red cherry on each scoop
• 5 sprinkles on each scoop

Dig into these questions:

1. How many + in all?

2. How many + altogether?

Here's the Scoop!

Glue the items on the plate in order:

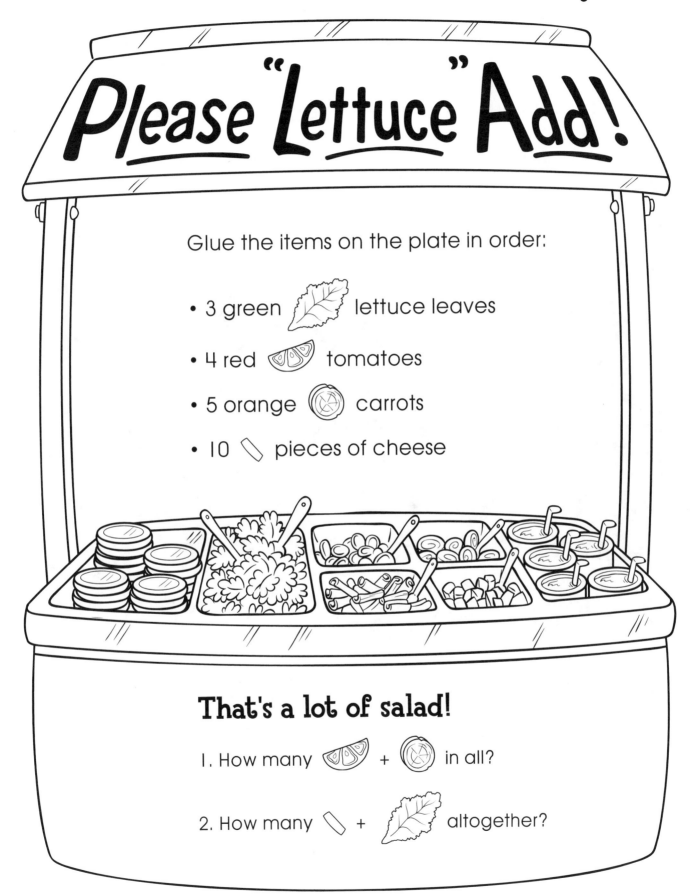

- 3 green lettuce leaves
- 4 red tomatoes
- 5 orange carrots
- 10 pieces of cheese

That's a lot of salad!

1. How many + in all?

2. How many + altogether?

Please "Lettuce" Add!

Glue the items on the pizza in order:

- 1 red of sauce
- 5 pink pepperoni slices
- 3 green peppers
- 2 gray mushrooms
- 10 pieces of cheese

You're cooKin' now!

1. How many + in all?

2. How many + in all?

Piecing Pizza Parts

Number Journals

Literature: *How Many, How Many, How Many*, by Rick Walton

Materials: Math journals, crayons or markers, chart paper and marker

Activity: Enthusiastic children will love shouting out answers to the rhyming number questions in *How Many, How Many, How Many*. This counting book poses queries about nursery rhymes, fairy tales, planets, seasons, and more. Because the story has students counting what they already know, it is the perfect springboard for your own classroom math journals.

Your students can keep an ongoing log of numbers and sets of objects one to twelve (or this activity may extend to higher numbers based on individual readiness). Begin by giving each child a small math journal. It saves a lot of time and confusion for the children later if the books are ready to go with each page featuring a numeral, number word, and corresponding dot(s). For example, page two would display the numeral "2," "two," and two dots. In addition, make a large class journal with chart paper to use as an example and to stimulate more ideas and discussion.

Encourage your students to be on the lookout for numbers and groups of objects everywhere. As you introduce and study the number two, for example, children might find two eyes, two mittens in winter, two characters in Jack and Jill, two gym shoes, and two lips. As students encounter these number sets, you can write them in the large class journal while students copy them in their math journals.

Because students are constantly looking for sets of numbers, you do not need to take time as a class to brainstorm "What items come in threes?" This abstract concept may be difficult for some young learners, but easier for others whom you can encourage to continue at their own pace and go as high as their interest allows. As the teacher, you can naturally keep the enthusiasm alive by taking a moment to count objects encountered in stories, in the hallways, on field trips, and so on, and add them to the class math journal periodically. At year's end, your mathematicians will have an impressive log of the numbers one through twelve and beyond!

Tongue Twisting Counts

Materials: Chart paper and marker or chalkboard and chart, paper and pencils

Activity: Teach alliteration to your students with these fun counting poems. Write the numerals 1–10, each on a separate sheet of chart paper. Tell the students that you want to create silly sentences for each number in which every word begins with the same sound as the number. Begin with the number one. Ask students to repeat the number. Brainstorm other words that begin with the same sound. They may respond with *whale*, *watch*, *white*, *woman*, or many other words. Write

Tongue Twisting Counts (cont.)

the correct responses on the number one chart. (Take the time to explain why some of the words they suggest may not belong on the chart. Continue in this fashion with the numbers up through ten.

Your students can create silly sentences from the words recorded on the charts. Depending on their ability, you may wish to continue the activity as a whole class, or you may assign pairs of students to work together. The sentences may be short and simple or long and complex. Here are two simple examples: "One whale wears a watch." "Two trees telephone teachers."

Some students may be ready to take this idea to a more difficult level. Encourage these students to create numbers with multiple digits, for example, 1,465. Have students again brainstorm words that begin with the same beginning sound and create a sentence in the same manner. For example, "One thousand four hundred sixty-five women wore white watches with their wigs when the wind worried them." (The word "and" is used only if there is a decimal in the number.)

After each student or pair of students has completed some silly sentences, each can be copied onto a large piece of construction paper and illustrated. Display these in a line (arrange them from greatest to least or least to greatest numbers, so students and visitors can practice counting, reading, and saying the number words while trying not to twist their tongues!

Digital Slide Show

Literature: *Let's Count,* by Tana Hoban; *Arlene Alda's 1 2 3* by Arlene Alda

Materials: Digital camera, materials for making booklets

Activity: Both *Let's Count*, by Tana Hoban, and *Arlene Alda's 1 2 3* offer children practice in counting while viewing stunning photography. *Let's Count* uses real-life photos of groups of items to represent each number. Your students can find or assemble groups of objects around the classroom and school yard to use in the slide show. Use a digital camera (remember to charge your battery in advance and have plenty of disks on hand) and take your students on a walk around the school building and school yard, reminding everyone to keep their eyes peeled for number sets. Snap shots of any they find (or allow your students to take the pictures) with the digital camera. (You may need to do some hunting before the children's walk so you know where to lead them, but remember to let them have the fun of actually finding the shot!)

Because you want each child to have a part in the activity, simply counting from one to ten may not offer enough opportunities. You can include more challenges if you encourage creativity in your students' counting. For example, ask students to skip count by threes, or to count from one to ten and then count by tens. Think of all the practice students will have counting when looking for the higher numbers of items!

You may want to create a theme book of numbers and photos. Seasons work very well as a topic since they are associated with so many recognizable symbols. In the fall, for example, students could take pictures of one jack-o'-lantern, two squirrels, three fallen leaves, four cornstalks, five apples, etc. A winter counting book could include mittens, scarves, hats, cups of hot cocoa, sleds, reindeer, snowflakes, etc. Who wouldn't love counting new flowers, worms on the sidewalk, umbrellas, butterflies, and rubber boots in the spring? With counting books, the possibilities are endless.

Later, when you have all the photos you need, load the disks into your computer and arrange the pictures in numerical order. Your students can type and narrate the counting on each picture. This step will take some time so you may want to have volunteers on hand or encourage your technology coordinator to participate with your class on this project. Run the finished slides as a continuous slide show and don't forget the popcorn!

Arlene Alda's 1 2 3 shows photos of objects in nature that resemble the numerals 1–10. Your students can make the same kind of counting book with a walk around the school yard and a digital camera. Review the photos in the book and note how the author used shapes in her surroundings for each number. Scissor handles resemble the number "9" and two bagel halves make an "8," for example. Brainstorm possibilities together and then go on a hunt! It may be fun to send small groups out to search with a volunteer so that the class will be surprised with what each group finds to represent its number. The end result can again be viewed as a slide show, or each page can be printed and copied so that each student receives a counting photo picture book created right in the school setting!

Hurray for One Hundred

Literature: *100 Days of School*, by Trudy Harris; *100 School Days*, by Anne Rockwell

Materials: Paper and pencils, crayons or markers, materials to make a class book

Activity: Many primary classrooms are teaching children to count to 100 by adding one number for every day they are in school. The celebration of learning is enjoyed once students have been in school for 100 days. While the process takes 100 days, many opportunities for learning occur along the way, such as patterning, counting by twos, fives, tens, and so on. Books such as *100 Days of School*, by Trudy Harris, and *100 School Days*, by Anne Rockwell, can be wonderful springboards to begin writing activities with your class.

After reading either of these books, encourage students to write number sentences with sums equaling 100. After verifying their equations for accuracy, challenge the students to identify the families of facts that correspond with the number sentences they have written. Give students time to illustrate their equations, encouraging them to be creative. Then, collect their work so that you may create a classroom book for all to enjoy.

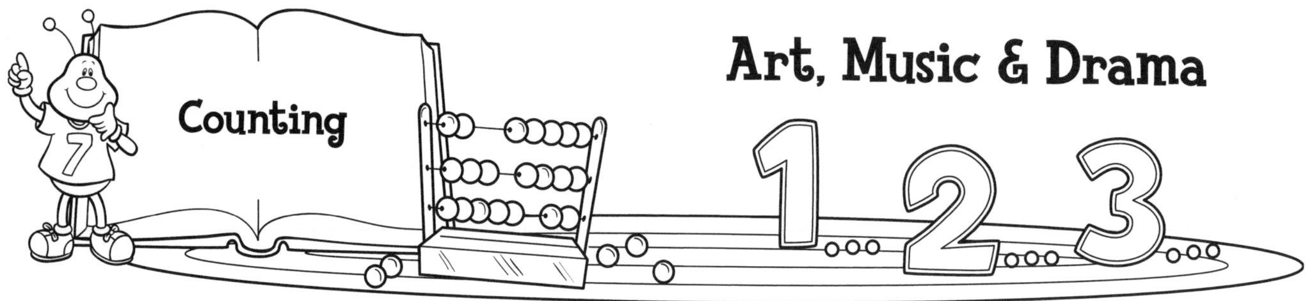

Puppets to Count On

Literature: *One Duck Stuck*, by Phyllis Root

Materials: Construction paper, crayons or markers, scissors, materials for decorating puppets (sequins, fabric scraps, ribbon, felt, buttons, glitter, etc.), craft sticks or rulers, masking tape

Activity: *One Duck Stuck*, by Phyllis Root, is a charming story that will capture your audience's attention with its vibrant illustrations, and hold that attention with its silly rhyme and sentence pattern. A duck gets stuck in the muddy marsh and his friends come by in groups numbering two through ten to help free him. Because of the rhythmic nature and variety of animal characters, *One Duck Stuck* would make a great puppet show. The repetitive lines are easy for students to read and reread, and they will also enjoy making the characters' silly animal sounds.

Read the story aloud several times to familiarize students with the large cast of characters and the language. There are ten different species in the book—one duck, two fish, three moose, etc.,—and you will also need a narrator. This all adds up to more than 50 parts, but the roles can be handled by any number of children. Assign two children to share the role of four crickets, for example. They can each design two crickets on one piece of paper and carry it as one puppet. Continue to fill the cast in this sharing manner.

Students can create their simple puppets with colored construction paper and crayons or markers. Encourage students to reflect the numbers being represented in the decoration of the puppets. For example, the nine snakes could have nine triangle designs and the ten dragonflies might have ten sequins on their wings. Your artists can add fun decorative touches with craft materials. Attach the finished puppets to rulers or craft sticks with masking tape.

Now your students are ready. Arm each puppeteer with a script and his puppet. Have the children wait quietly "offstage," entering only when it is their turn to speak. Encourage students to wiggle their puppets as they speak so the audience knows which puppet is "talking."

Extension: You may choose to stage performances and invite parents to an entire afternoon of counting fun. Invitations can be created by the students and might include the top 10 reasons to attend. The room, of course, could be decorated with scores of counting projects. Have the class counting books proudly read aloud. Count on parents to be terrifically entertained!

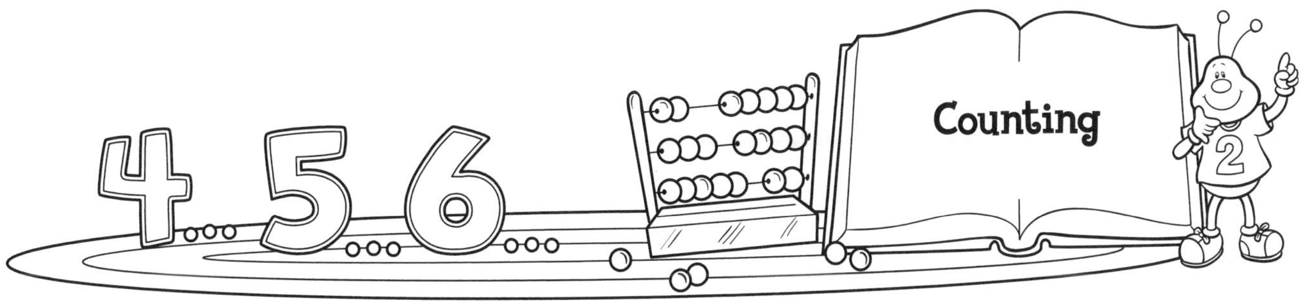

Quick Quilting

Literature: *One Moose, Twenty Mice*, by Clare Beaton

Materials: Construction paper, pencils, crayons or markers, scissors, glue

Activity: *One Moose, Twenty Mice* has unique illustrations that look like felt pieces cut and sewn into animal characters. Young readers will enjoy searching for the cat that is hidden on each page. Invite your students to make a counting quilt. Divide the class into small groups. Assign each group a number and instruct the students to make construction-paper animals that have the corresponding number of pieces glued to them. (For example, if a small group has the number three, students need to work together to create three animals, such as turkeys. The three turkeys should also reflect the number three by having three feathers and three spots on their tummies.) Your task is to create one animal to hide in all the square designs like the cat in *One Moose, Twenty Mice*. A class pet would be a perfect choice.

Variation: For a special keepsake, have students work with real felt pieces, adding the correct number of craft jewels, feathers, buttons, and so on. Then have each group glue its animals to one quilt square of fabric. Ask a parent volunteer to sew the squares together beginning with the number one, then two, and so on to create a quiltlike banner.

Monkey Business

Literature: *Five Little Monkeys Jumping on the Bed*, retold and illustrated by Eileen Christelow

Materials: Two toy telephones (optional)

Activity: *Five Little Monkeys Jumping on the Bed* is a story that many children know, and it can make an active choral reading lesson. Students will enjoy acting out the backward counting and various characters portrayed in the book. Select five students to come to the front of the classroom and jump up and down as if on a bed. Choose two more students, one to be the mother who calls the doctor and the other to act as the stern doctor. Begin with five monkeys, but increase the level of difficulty as your students understand the concept. Eventually, all of the little monkeys in the classroom will be jumping up and down. Conclude the activity by having students counting backward until just one little monkey is left on the bed. It will be especially fun to dramatize the falling out of bed, but be sure to emphasize safety not silliness. Providing the mother and doctor with play telephones is another touch that will make this a favorite counting backward activity!

Digit Designers

Literature: *Way Out in the Desert*, by T. J. Marsh and Jennifer Ward

Materials: Paper, pencils, crayons and markers

Activity: *Way Out in the Desert*, which is based on the traditional "Over in the Meadow," introduces children of all ages to desert animals and their habitats. The illustrations will entertain young readers as they try to find a hidden numeral on each colorful page and match it by finding the corresponding number of animals on the page.

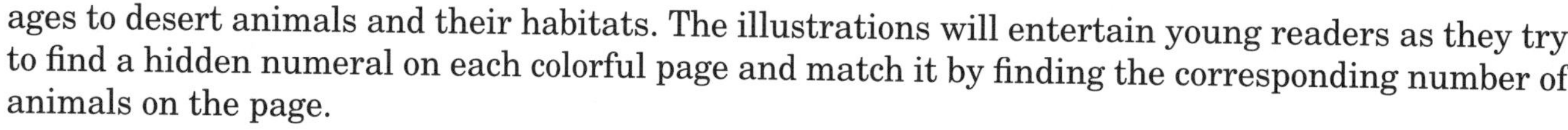

Encourage your students to became authors and illustrators while they review numerals and number word matching. Write numbers, one on each small piece of paper for as many students as are in your class (e.g., 1–25, if there are 25 students in the classroom). Students can select a number from a hat or, if you know you have some students who will struggle with this activity, you may want to give them lower numbers and assign your accelerated students the higher numbers to challenge them.

Ask your students to select a habitat in which to have the book take place. If you are studying oceans, for example, you may want to choose that habitat. Have students brainstorm to a list of animals that would be seen in the ocean.

Now the fun can begin! Using math skills and artistic talents, students can create their pages for the class book. Encourage students to illustrate their pages with scenes of the habitat they selected. Before they color their completed illustrations, have them hide the corresponding numeral somewhere in the scene. (For example, a page from an ocean book may have the numeral 16 hidden in the scene and 16 seastars drawn on the sandy bottom of the ocean.) As you assess their work, you can easily identify those students that have a good understanding of number recognition. Invite students to collate the book pages in the correct sequence once all of the pages are completed.

Chocolate-Candy Cookies

Literature: *The M&M's Brand Counting Book*, by Barbara Barbieri McGrath

Materials: Individual packs of candy-coated chocolate pieces, prepared cookie dough (or cookie dough ingredients), cookie sheet, oven, oven mitts

Activity: Provide students with individual packs of candies and let them know they will be completing an activity before they eat them. Have your mathematicians sort the candies into colored sets. Students can then arrange the candies into bar graphs on their desktops from most to least. Then, ask students to provide assistance in mixing cookie dough, or you may choose to purchase the prepared dough available in the refrigerated section of the grocery store. After students have washed their hands, give each student a chunk of the dough, enough to make one cookie. Assign a number to each student and have him place that number of candies on his cookie. Bake the cookies and place them in numerical order. Practice counting the candies again as the students eat their delicious math manipulatives! To challenge students, count each candy as five to practice counting by fives, then repeat, counting by tens.

Estimation Imagination

Materials: Clear plastic jar, individually wrapped candy pieces

Activity: Transform a clear plastic container into an estimation jar. Each week fill the jar with treats and encourage your students to estimate how many pieces are in the container. At the end of each week, students can help count the number of treats inside the jar. Whose estimate was the closest? Is there an easier way to count bigger numbers, perhaps by fives or tens?

Because it can become costly to provide a jar full of treats each week, you may choose to ask students to take turns taking the plastic container home and filling it with edible items. You may want to send a letter to parents/guardians, explaining the directions, purpose, and goals of this activity.

Paper Bag Puppets

Literature: *My Little Sister Ate One Hare*, by Bill Grossman

Materials: Paper lunch bags, crayons or markers, decorative materials (construction paper, craft materials, etc.), scissors, glue, candy pieces or healthful snacks to serve as counters

Activity: Children love to hear disgusting facts and anecdotes, and this hilarious tale certainly delivers the gross factor. *My Little Sister Ate One Hare*, by Bill Grossman, is a cumulative story in which a little girl eats too much, first one thing, then two, then three, and so on, until she reaches ten. Eventually, she throws up. Read it aloud once to share the humor. Read it aloud again to practice counting. While you are rereading the story, children can count along with you and "feed" their own little sister paper bag puppets.

To make the paper bag puppet, each child needs a paper lunch bag and some coloring materials. With the open end at the top, the child should decorate the bag to resemble a little girl. You may choose to cut a large mouth hole in each paper bag, or simply use the opening at the top of the bag.

Next, give each child plenty of candy counters to feed her puppet. As you read page one, have your students feed one counter to their puppets. She is fed two counters as you read what the little sister eats on page two, and so on. You may use jellybeans, candy corn, marshmallows, cereal pieces, raisins, nutritious snacks, or other plentiful items as your counters. (*Note:* Check for food allergies.) If you use a variety of healthful items, your students could enjoy a snack of trail mix as you reach the story's conclusion.

Number Order with Baseballs

Literature: *The Baseball Counting Book*, by Barbara Barbieri McGrath

Materials: Backpack or tote bag, copy of the book, 2 egg cartons, 20 table tennis balls, resealable plastic bag (large enough to hold the table tennis balls), parent letter (reproducible, page 31), black permanent marker, red permanent marker (optional), blank booklets or notebooks (optional)

Activity: Your children will love hearing *The Baseball Counting Book* by Barbara Barbieri McGrath. Two teams play the all-American pastime while counting to twenty. From two teams and three strikes to nineteen ice cream cones celebrating the win, students will enjoy the rhyming text and lively illustrations! Share their enthusiasm with parents by creating a backpack or tote bag that includes the story and activities to send home.

To prepare the counting activity, first use a black permanent marker to number the table tennis balls from 1 through 20 (a red permanent marker could be used to add stitching lines to make them resemble baseballs) and store them in the plastic bag. Finally, put the two egg cartons, the "baseballs," a copy of the book, and a copy of the letter to parents from page 31 in the backpack.

At home, with help from parents, students will reread the story (or listen to it). Then, they can pull the numbered balls from the bag, name the numbers aloud, and place the balls in numerical order in the egg cartons. Your young learners will get lots of practice counting as they try to find each numbered ball its rightful place in the egg cartons. This fun counting and ordering activity should score a home run with parents and students!

Variation: You may want to include a blank booklet in the backpack and encourage rookie writers to create their own version of a counting book. Once illustrations and an "All about the Author" page are completed as well as the counting text, young authors can return their books to school to share with the class to receive scores of applause from their fans!

Buggy about Counting

Literature: *Ten Little Ladybugs*, by Melanie Gerth

Materials: Backpack or tote bag, 10 plastic toy ladybugs or other bugs, resealable plastic bag, 2 dice, box of crayons, ladybug pattern (reproducible, page 33), parent letter (reproducible, page 32), copy of *Ten Little Ladybugs*

Activity: Children should enjoy both hearing and touching the *Ten Little Ladybugs*. Plastic ladybugs and rhyming text will help your students identify the number of insects left after one flies away on each page. They will get lots of practice counting backwards from ten as they read and reread this story with family members at home and complete several follow-up activities.

In a backpack or tote, send home the storybook, a bag of ten plastic bugs, ladybug activity sheet, two dice, and a box of crayons. Encourage parents to help their child reread the story and count the leftover ladybugs on each page. When the story is over, the children can continue counting with the bugs from the bag. The bugs will serve as manipulatives to aid the child in counting both forward and backward.

Next, have the child decorate the ladybugs' wings on the coloring sheet. She should roll both dice to determine the total number of spots to be drawn on each wing on the first ladybug. The student can then color black dots on one wing to match the number rolled on one die, while the other wing should match the other die. This step is repeated for the second ladybug on the activity sheet.

Students ready for higher numbers can roll the two dice and add the numbers together to get one wing numeral and then repeat the process to get the numeral for the other wing. Be sure the student includes the number sentence for the sum. Students can finish coloring each ladybug any way they wish. When the decorated ladybugs are returned, hang them on a bulletin board entitled "Buggy about Numbers!"

Variation: Students can easily assemble their own construction paper ladybugs to decorate rather than using a simple coloring sheet. All you need for each bug are two circles: one large red circle for the body and one small black circle for the head. Draw a line down the center of the red circle to make two wings and glue the head to the back of the red circle. It can be that simple. Of course, students can also embellish their bugs with antennae, legs, and a face. At home, they can either draw and color black spots, or cut them out of construction paper and attach them with a glue stick.

All Buddies Count!

Literature: *Every Buddy Counts*, by Stuart J. Murphy

Materials: Construction paper, parent letter (reproducible, page 31)

Activity: *Every Buddy Counts*, by Stuart J. Murphy, allows us to follow a little girl's journey, in which she counts all of her buddies from one to ten. She has one hamster, two sisters, and ten teddy bears to snuggle at night. Encourage your students to recognize the important friends in their lives (and notice that the number of friends well exceeds 10) with this take-home project.

Begin by giving each child a large piece of construction paper made to look like a chart, with two columns of five boxes each for a total of ten. Each student is to take the chart home along with a copy of the parent letter on page 31, and use both pictures and words to show one to ten buddies in groups. Ask parents to attach a photo of the child to the center of the chart. When the students bring in the completed posters, allow time for sharing. Display the posters around the room as a visual reminder of both numbers and of how rich in buddies they all are!

Challenge students to determine the total number of buddies on their charts. Students may write their totals (such as 55) on the backs of the charts so as not to give the answer away!

One to 100 Ways to Help at Home

Literature: *One Hundred Hungry Ants*, by Elinor J. Pinczes

Materials: Copy of the storybook, parent letter from page 32, cards or papers each containing one number, construction paper, glue, decorative items (optional), materials to bind the class book

Activity: *One Hundred Hungry Ants*, by Elinor J. Pinczes, is a book that takes ants from one to one hundred. Send home the book, along with an assigned number from the book. (Be sure to give each student a different number, higher numbers for students who are ready for the challenge and lower numbers for students still mastering counting skills. If appropriate, you may consider sending home multiples of fives, all even numbers, etc.)

Family members can assist in the learning process by creating a number page with their child. After they have read the story together, they will construct their own number page on a large piece of colored construction paper. Students begin by hunting around the house for small items to glue on their number pages. They can use cotton balls, cereal pieces, buttons, stickers, or craft pom-poms. Parents and students will have fun choosing unique objects to personalize their page. If you suspect this will be a problem for a family, feel free to include a bag of items for decorating the page.

Once all the students have had a chance to complete a page, assemble the number pages in numerical order. Make a cover for the book and enjoy reading and counting the found objects together as a class. You do not need to worry about any missing numbered pages, just count your way from one page to the next numbered page. For example, suppose page thirteen is complete and the next completed page is twenty-four. While you turn the page ask students to verbally count along with you—13, 14, 15 . . .—until you reach the number on the next page.

One to 100 Ways to Help at Home (cont.)

Extension: You may want to include some additional activities that parents can do with their children at home to reinforce counting! Here are some ideas:

- *Place Value Review:* Ask students to identify tens and ones place value in numbers in the book. This can be done by simply including the reproducible on page 34, on which students write the tens digit in black in the tens column and the ones digit in red in the ones column.
- *Anticipation of Ants:* Students can continue to write numbers beyond 100 on a blank booklet page included in the bag that is sent home. Encourage students to write the number and word and then draw an illustration that includes that number of black ants on the page. For example, a child may choose to illustrate 135. In this case, she would write the "135" and "one hundred thirty-five" and color 135 black ants. Once the pages are complete, assemble the pages in numerical order to make a class booklet. Encourage the students to select a title for the booklet, for example "More Than 100!"
- *Reciting for Review:* For students who are struggling with the skill, parents can help their children practice counting by encouraging them to use their index fingers to point to each item as they count.
- *Counting Cards:* Parents can assist students learning to count by playing a card game. Divide a standard deck of cards into even piles, one for each player. Taking turns, each player tries to play the card next in the counting sequence. For example, player one plays a one (ace) card of any suit, player two needs to pass or play a two card of any suit, the next player passes or plays the three and so on. The winner will be the first player out of cards. This card game lends itself nicely to a station in the classroom as well. (If students are confused by the face cards, you may remove these from the deck. Alternatively, use a deck of cards from a card game that shows only numerals.)
- *What and Where:* This game can be played at home like the familiar "I Spy" game. One player says, "I see something in this room and there is only one." The other players take turns guessing the items, for instance, one television. The player who guesses correctly the mystery item identifies the object for the number two. He says, "I see something in this room and there are only two." In this case, there may be two candlesticks or two pillows on the couch. The players continue guessing what and where for as many objects as they can.

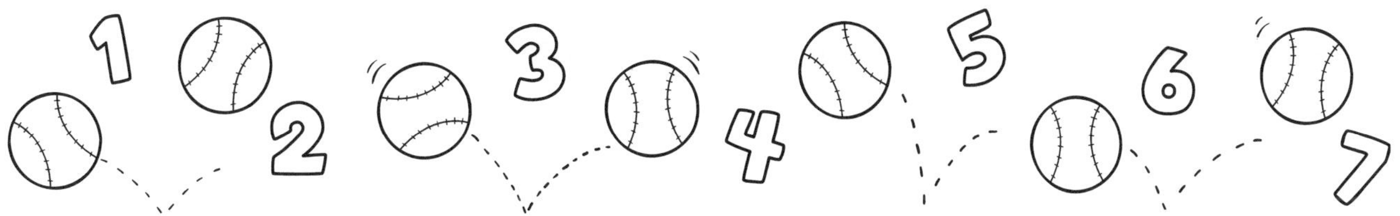

Dear Parents,

Hit a grand slam by assisting your child with this counting backpack! Enclosed you'll find *The Baseball Counting Book*, two egg cartons, and twenty numbered balls. Read about the all-American pastime while counting to 20 with your child. Your child may want to read to you or you can take turns reading aloud. Next, monitor your child as he or she removes the balls and places them in numerical order in the egg cartons. This counting and ordering activity is sure to score a home run!

Please return all materials to school by ____________________. Thank you for your continued support and cooperation.

Sincerely,

Dear Parents,

As you know, we are counting in math class. At the same time, we want to recognize the important people in our lives. Your child can accomplish both with this at-home project. We read a book, *Every Buddy Counts*, in which the main character counts all of her friends. She has one hamster, two sisters, and so on, up to ten teddy bears to snuggle at night.

Your child is to make a poster using illustrations, pictures, and words to help him/her count, from one to ten, the groups of friends around him or her. The friends may be real people in your family or neighborhood or animals, real or stuffed. Each box is numbered with the amount of friends to feature in that box. To begin, please help your child put his or her picture in the center of the poster. Finally, have your child count all the buddies on the poster and put the total number on the back of the poster.

We will share these posters in class on ____________________. The poster will be returned safely home to you after the display is taken down. Thank you very much for your assistance in this special project. What a great reminder of how rich in friends we all are!

Sincerely,

Buggy about Counting

Dear Parents,

Our class is going buggy about counting! We have recently read *Ten Little Ladybugs* and are anxious to use it to practice counting. You can reread this delightful story with your child any number of ways. You can read it aloud, your child can read to you, or you can read it aloud together, taking turns. Once the story is finished, encourage your child to count forward and backward using the plastic bugs. For example, your child can begin with 5, 3, or 7 and continue counting on.

Next, your child may color and decorate the ladybug picture with the crayons provided. Have your child roll the dice to determine the number of spots on each wing. One die is the number of spots your child should color on one wing, and the second die is for the other wing. Repeat this step for the second ladybug. Your child can finish coloring the bugs as desired.

Please send all the materials back to me by ______________________________.

Thank you for your support. I'm glad I can count on you!

Sincerely,

One to 100 Ways to Help at Home

Dear Parents,

I know we can *count* on you to help us practice counting! *One Hundred Hungry Ants* will help, too! After you have finished reading the book aloud, encourage your child to design a number page for a class booklet. Your child's number is: ______________.

To complete the number page, you are going to need small items that can be glued on the large sheet of construction paper. Your child can use cotton balls, cereal pieces, buttons, stickers, or maybe even craft pom-poms. Be creative and use whatever you have lying around.

This project is due ____________________________. I appreciate your time and support with this project, and I know your child will be chanting, "You're number one!"

Sincerely,

Ladybug Pattern

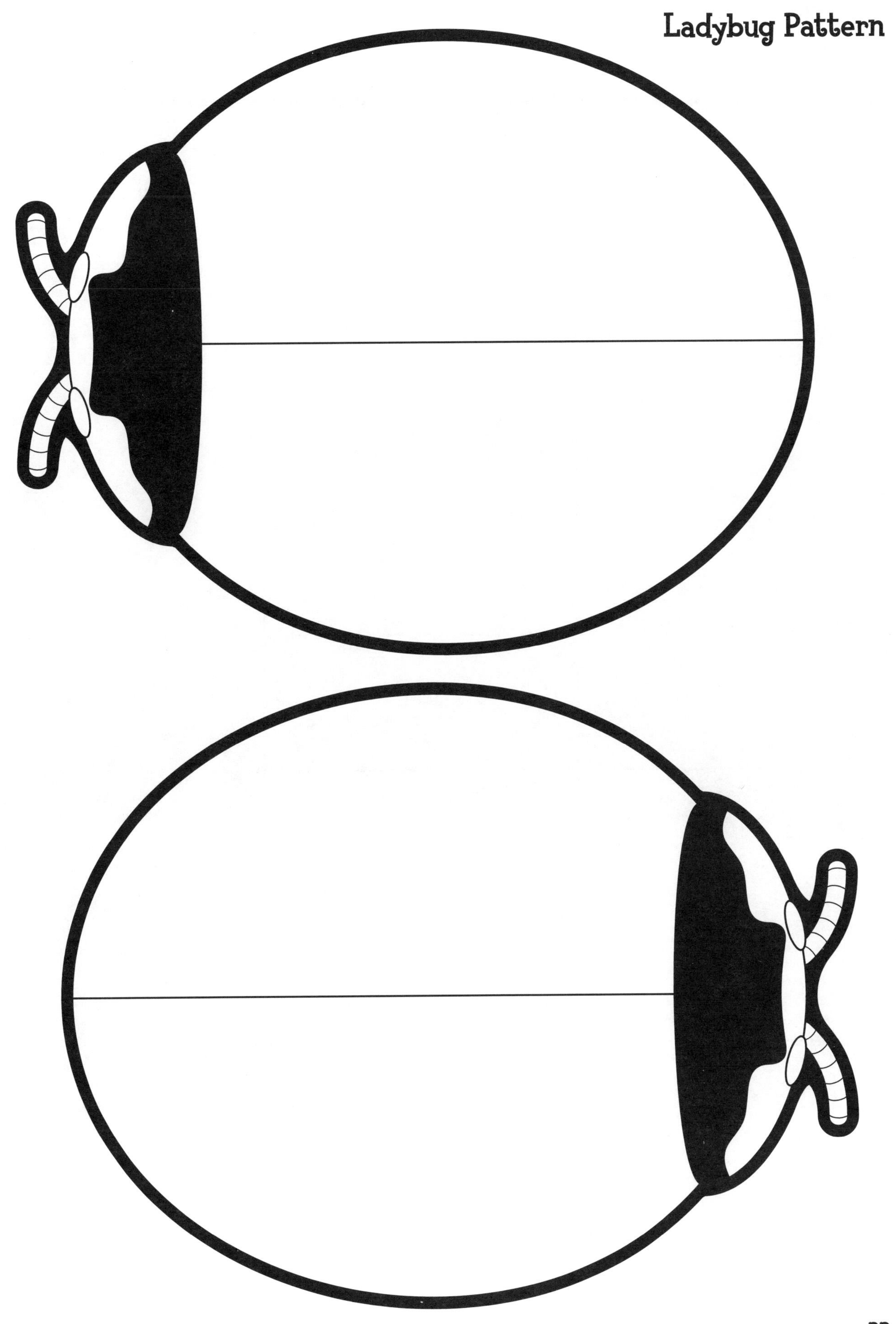

Name: ______________________________ Date: ______________

Place Value Review

Directions: Write the numbers from the storybook in the Standard Number column. Then tell how many tens and ones are in each number.

Standard Number	Tens	Ones

Shapes and Patterns

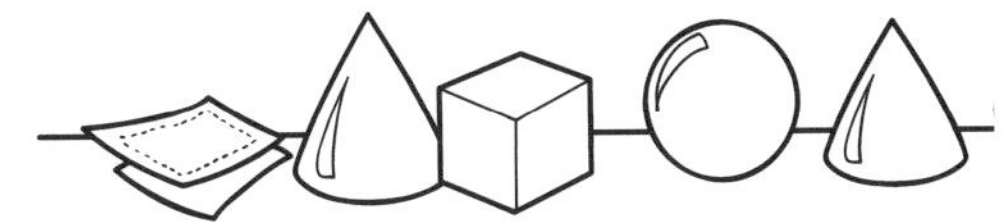

Learning about basic shapes helps children in their discovery of the world around them and lays a foundation for later math skills. Have fun with these projects based on shapes and books!

Shapes and Patterns

Language Arts (page 38)

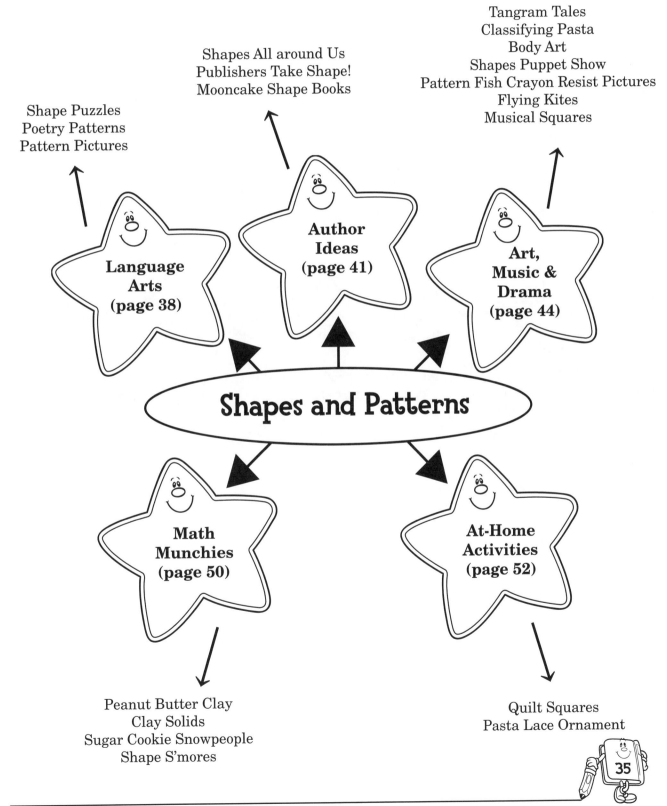

Shape Puzzles
Poetry Patterns
Pattern Pictures

Author Ideas (page 41)

Shapes All around Us
Publishers Take Shape!
Mooncake Shape Books

Art, Music & Drama (page 44)

Tangram Tales
Classifying Pasta
Body Art
Shapes Puppet Show
Pattern Fish Crayon Resist Pictures
Flying Kites
Musical Squares

Math Munchies (page 50)

Peanut Butter Clay
Clay Solids
Sugar Cookie Snowpeople
Shape S'mores

At-Home Activities (page 52)

Quilt Squares
Pasta Lace Ornament

Literature Selections

Featured Literature

The following selections are used in conjunction with the activities in this section. You may want to obtain them from your library before you start the unit. (Activities with which the books are used are listed in parentheses.)

The Boy and the Quilt, by Shirley Kurtz (Good Books, 1991). A young boy demonstrates an interest in quilting. Rhyme and general quilting instructions make this a great book for young quilters. (Quilt Squares, page 52)

Cubes, Cones, Cylinders & Spheres, by Tana Hoban (Greenwillow Books, 2000). Solids are all around us, taking shape as familiar objects. This is the concept of this wordless book of photography. (Clay Solids, page 50)

Fun with Shapes, by Peter Patilla (Millbrook Press, 1998). Colorful illustrations with probing questions in simple text help students understand the functions of different shapes. The author also uses perspective to help children see shapes from a different viewpoint. (Musical Squares, page 47)

Grandfather Tang's Story, by Ann Tompert (Crown Publishers, 1990). Tompert uses tangrams to show the shape of each character she introduces into this Chinese folktale. A pattern for the tangrams is included at the end of the book so that teachers and students can create their own pictures. (Tangram Tales, page 44)

The Greedy Triangle, by Marilyn Burns (Scholastic, 1994). A greedy triangle asks neighbors and friends to add lines and angles to explore different shapes. (Shapes Puppet Show, page 45; Peanut Butter Clay, page 50)

Let's Fly a Kite, by Stuart J. Murphy (HarperCollins Publishers, 2000). Two children learn about symmetry one day when they make and decorate a kite. Murphy incorporates explanatory information throughout the story to teach the concept of symmetrical figures. (Flying Kites, page 46)

Pattern Fish, by Trudy Harris (Millbrook Press, Inc., 2000). This book illustrates patterns in the borders, pictures, and text. Students will enjoy trying to identify the patterns they see and hear. (Pattern Pictures, page 39; Pattern Fish Crayon Resist Pictures, page 46)

Round Is a Mooncake, by Roseanne Thong (Chronicle Books, 2000). Thong uses bright pictures and easy rhyming text to illustrate shapes found in everyday things. A brief explanation of the cultural items found in the story is included at the end of the book. (Mooncake Shape Books, page 42)

The Shape of Things, by Janine Scott (Compass Point Books, 2003). This book is set up like a miniature textbook for young mathematicians with a table of contents, glossary, and a bibliographical reference list in terms students can read and understand. Attributes and examples are given for many shapes. (Publishers Take Shape! page 41)

Shapes, Shapes, Shapes, by Tana Hoban (Greenwillow Books, 1986). This wordless book uses photographs of life in the city to portray different shapes. (Body Art, page 45)

The Silly Story of Goldie Locks and the Three Squares, by Grace Maccarone (Scholastic, 1996). Maccarone uses the classic children's favorite and adds humor and the mathematical concept of shapes in her own variation. (Classifying Pasta, page 44)

So Many Circles, So Many Squares, by Tana Hoban (Greenwillow Books, 1998). Hoban uses photographs of everyday objects to identify circles and squares. This wordless picture book is a resource to use to reinforce shapes with young learners. (Shape Puzzles, page 38; Shapes All around Us, page 41)

Additional Suggested Literature

Circles, by Jan Kottke (Welcome Books, 2000). This book explores circles in photographs and easy-to-read text. Guided questions accompany each illustration to foster class discussion about circles in a machine, circles that shine, circles that tell time, and more.

Color Farm, by Lois Ehlert (Lippincott, 1990). Ehlert uses rhyme, shapes, and colors to explore the different animals found on a farm. Each animal is one layer of shape cutouts, and each shape is clearly identified on the opposite page.

Eye Spy Shapes, by Debbie MacKinnon (Charlesbridge, 2000). This peephole book offers young children an introduction to shapes in a vast array of objects easily recognized by the reader.

Sea Shapes, by Suse MacDonald (Voyager Books, 1994). As students pore over each page depicting a different underwater creature, they are encouraged to find a variety of shapes. The illustrations were created by cutting the objects from paper to fashion an ocean scene.

A Star in My Orange: Looking for Nature's Shapes, by Dana Meachen Rau (Millbrook Press, 2002). Beautiful photography and uncomplicated text are used to encourage the reader to look for all types of shapes in nature.

Three Pigs, One Wolf, and Seven Magic Shapes, by Grace Maccarone (Scholastic, 1997). Maccarone has produced a variation of the three pigs story using tangram shapes for various purposes.

Word Bird's Shapes, by Jane Belk Moncure (Child's World, 2003). Simple text and bright colors lead beginning readers through a lesson in making pictures using a variety of shapes. Several tangram pictures are included at the book's conclusion.

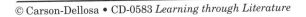

Shape Puzzles

Literature: *So Many Circles, So Many Squares*, by Tana Hoban

Materials: Disposable cameras, rulers, scissors, envelopes, pencils and paper

Students love taking pictures. Introduce Tana Hoban's photography with the book *So Many Circles, So Many Squares*. After you have shared the photographs and talked about the shapes, divide the class into small groups. Give each group a disposable camera and take some time to explain how to operate the cameras. Allow students an opportunity to look through the lens and locate the buttons.

Next, accompany the groups as they go out into the school or school yard to find shapes in the things they see. For example, they could take a picture of the circle found in the clock on the wall. Each student should take two or three pictures in case the photo is out of focus or the shape is cut off. When you develop the film, it might be a wise idea to get double prints so that you have extra pictures for students that need a bit more practice with the camera.

After you have developed the film, let each student select one photograph to create a puzzle. Cut it into nine squares by using a ruler to draw a simple tic-tac-toe diagram on the back. Give each student an envelope for storing the puzzle pieces. Students can write a short riddle describing the shape or the place shown in the photo. (Example: "I am short but I am strong. People use me all day long. I'm not a triangle. I'm not square. I fill up fast and keep the area clear. What am I?" — trash can, circle)

Poetry Patterns

Materials: Chart paper, construction paper shapes, markers, crayons, small rubber stamps and ink pad, reproducible (page 40)

Activity: Even the simplest rhyming poetry demonstrates language patterns. Use poetry as a springboard for identifying patterns and immerse your students into poems that will relate to any unit of study across the curriculum. Select several simple poems that have a rhyming pattern. Write each poem on chart paper and then encourage your students to try to identify the rhyming pattern that the poet has chosen. Once students have determined the pattern, use construction paper shapes such as circles, squares, or triangles to identify each line of the poem. For example, if the poem demonstrates an ABAB pattern, place circles next to the "A" lines and squares next to the "B" lines. Then, let students practice this skill by identifying the patterns in the other poems. Students can use markers or crayons to draw different colored shapes by each line, or you can provide small stamps for them to use. Use the lines from "Twinkle, Twinkle, Little Star" (page 40) to reinforce this concept.

Pattern Pictures

Literature: *Pattern Fish*, by Trudy Harris

Materials: Construction paper, writing paper, glue, small bowls or resealable plastic bags of breakfast cereal representing different shapes, pencils

Activity: Students are often more successful with a concept when they can use manipulatives. Your students may enjoy creating these pattern pictures and practicing their writing skills as well. Read the book *Pattern Fish*, by Trudi Harris. Point out the patterns that Harris has included in the borders on each page. Then, give each student a piece of construction paper, a smaller piece of writing paper, glue, and a small bowl or plastic bag of breakfast cereal pieces that are different shapes and/or colors. Instruct your students to use the cereal to create a patterned border on the construction paper by placing the cereal pieces on the outside edges of the paper. When they are satisfied with their patterns, tell them to apply a line of glue along one edge of the paper. Then they may carefully place each piece of cereal on the glue. Have students complete each side of their borders the same way. When they have glued the cereal along each edge of their papers, they may set their borders aside to dry. While the cereal borders are drying, have the students use the smaller sheets of paper to describe their patterns in words. If your students can write sentences, remind them to include capital letters and punctuation. Students who are not able to write sentences may simply write the names of the shapes or colors the pattern demonstrates.

Name: ______________________ Date: ______________

Poetry Patterns

Directions: Read the following poem silently. See if you can find the rhyming pattern in the lines. Then use crayons to mark the pattern.

_____ Twinkle, twinkle, little star,

_____ How I wonder what you are.

_____ Up above the world so high,

_____ Like a diamond in the sky.

_____ Twinkle, twinkle, little star,

_____ How I wonder what you are.

Shapes All around Us

Literature: *So Many Circles, So Many Squares*, by Tana Hoban

Materials: Digital camera, presentation software

Activity: Once children are familiar with basic shapes, they will begin to see them in everyday objects. You can reinforce this identification process with Tana Hoban's book, *So Many Circles, So Many Squares*. Hoban uses photographs to capture circles and squares in this wordless picture book. Share the book with your students. Then, take a walk around your school with a digital camera. See what kinds of shapes your students can identify in the things they see every day. Take pictures of the shapes they point out. For example, students might recognize a square in the window of the principal's door or a circle in the basketball hoop in the gymnasium. They might even begin to see other shapes, such as a rectangle in the bookshelves in the library or a triangle in a sandwich cut in two. Once you've taken 15 or 20 pictures with the digital camera, import them into presentation software on the computer that will allow you to create a slide show. Alternatively, print out each picture and assemble a classroom book of photographs just like Hoban's.

Publishers Take Shape!

Literature: *The Shape of Things*, by Janine Scott

Materials: Booklet page (reproducible, page 43), construction paper, stapler, crayons or markers

Activity: Your mathematicians will be eager to create their own booklets after reading *The Shape of Things*, by Janine Scott. This uncomplicated book describes many familiar shapes and captures examples of each in photographs. Encourage your students to do the same with their own booklets made with copies of page 43 stapled with construction paper covers.

While you create example pages on the chalkboard, student can follow along and work in their own booklets. For example, draw a large square on page 1 and write "square" on the line. Direct students to look around the room searching for squares. Do they see any squares? They may respond with windows, floor tiles, calendar blocks, books, etc. Choose one of the examples and make a simple drawing of it on the facing page. If appropriate, students can add a sentence or two defining the attributes of each shape. For example: A square has four equal sides. Each page will only take a few minutes, and in no time these handy references will take shape!

Mooncake Shape Books

Literature: *Round Is a Mooncake*, by Roseanne Thong

Materials: Paper, scissors, hole punch, brad fasteners, crayons or markers

Activity: Roseanne Thong uses Asian culture to explore shapes found in the moon, lanterns, rice bowls, and other objects in her book, *Round Is a Mooncake*. Share the book with your class and talk about the shapes that the author finds in everyday objects. Then, give your students an opportunity to demonstrate their understanding of shapes by creating their own books.

First, as a class decide what shape the books should be. Then, cut out five identical shapes from paper for each booklet. Make sure the shapes are large enough for a simple sentence and a corresponding picture. Stack the circular-shaped (or whatever shape has been selected) pages together and punch a hole through the pages. Then use a brad to fasten them together so they can rotate around to reveal each new page. Now the book is ready for a student to create a title page and four pages that describe that shape. Students can write about and illustrate their four pages with everyday objects that have the chosen shape. Encourage them to follow the format of *Round is a Mooncake*.

Example: Title: Round Is a Sun

Page 1: Round is a bicycle wheel.

Page 2: Round is a basketball.

Page 3: Round is a hamburger.

Page 4: Round is a cherry pie.

This is a ______________

(Draw the shape.)

I can see this shape in . . .

Tangram Tales

Literature: *Grandfather Tang's Story*, by Ann Tompert

Materials: Tangram pattern (reproducible, page 48), scissors, self-adhesive magnet tape, colored paper, glue

Activity: Introduce different shapes to your students using tangrams. A tangram begins with a square, which is cut into seven pieces. Each piece, or tan, is used to create a picture.

Use the patterns on page 48 to share this traditional Chinese puzzle with your students. Reproduce the large pattern and cut out the tans to use on the chalkboard by adding a magnet to the back of each piece. Discuss the shapes with the students and give them an opportunity to identify them as triangles, squares, parallelograms, etc. Read Ann Tompert's book, *Grandfather Tang's Story*, to your students and create each character by arranging the tans. Then give each student a set of tans to manipulate into different pictures. After they have had some time to practice arranging the shapes, give each child a sheet of colored paper to which she can glue a completed tangram. More advanced students may want to add background illustrations to their tangrams. Proudly display these shape creations on a bulletin board.

Classifying Pasta

Literature: *The Silly Story of Goldie Locks and the Three Squares*, by Grace Maccarone

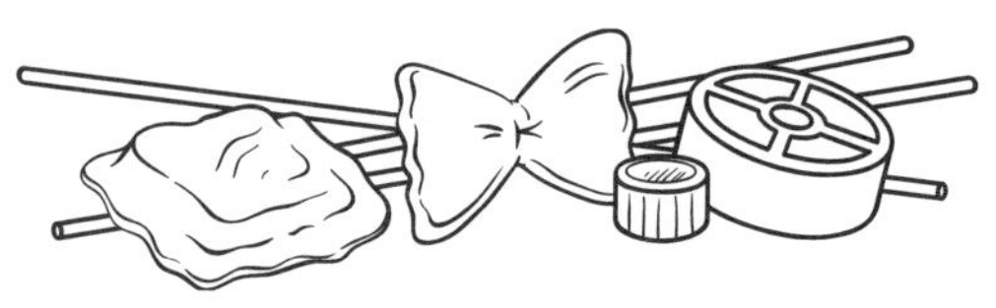

Materials: Pasta in a variety of shapes, resealable plastic bags, construction paper, glue, tempera paint, paintbrushes, scissors, reproducible on page 49

Activity: Many children can identify basic shapes like circles, squares, and triangles, but it is not uncommon for students to become confused with irregular polygons. One good book that demonstrates the idea that geometric figures can come in all different shapes and sizes is Grace Maccarone's book, *The Silly Story of Goldie Locks and the Three Squares*.

After reading the story, use pasta to categorize shapes. An easy way to do this is to put a variety of uncooked pasta into small plastic bags. Let students work in small groups to categorize the shapes of the pasta. For example, wagon wheels would be classified as circles, spaghetti would be classified as lines, bow-tie pasta (broken in half) could be classified as triangles, etc. Provide glue and tempera paint and invite students to glue the shapes in their categories onto the construction paper and paint them. To reinforce the idea that geometric shapes are not always created with equal sides, let students use the reproducible on page 49 to add additional shapes to their papers. Simply have them cut out the shapes and glue them onto their papers in the correct categories.

Body Art

Literature: *Shapes, Shapes, Shapes*, by Tana Hoban

Materials: Digital camera and software (optional)

Activity: Forms and figures really begin to take shape with this flexible activity! Begin by reviewing shapes with the wordless book *Shapes, Shapes, Shapes*, by Tana Hoban. Next, get your students moving around by having them create basic shapes with their bodies. Take this activity outside on a dry sunny day or move to an inside area with lots of floor space. Informally group your students by four. As you call out each shape, direct each group to lie on the ground or floor to form the shape. Groups of four can work cooperatively to create a square, circle, oval, rectangle, diamond, or even a trapezoid or rhombus. When forming a triangle, one member can stand up and be the director.

You can take this lesson one step further by taking digital pictures of your dramatic student forms. Arrange the pictures into a digital slide show and add text or student voices. Watching the video will provide an exciting review before assessment time!

Shapes Puppet Show

Literature: *The Greedy Triangle*, by Marilyn Burns

Materials: Puppet-making materials (craft sticks, construction paper, glue, scissors, fabric scraps, etc.), large sheets of construction paper, crayons or markers, old magazines and catalogs (optional)

Activity: Get your students into the act with a "shapes puppet show." *The Greedy Triangle*, by Marilyn Burns, is a perfect introduction for your young performers. After reading about a triangle who tries on many different shapes, your young thespians will be ready to show what they know!

Assign each student a shape (duplicates are okay) and provide them with puppet-making materials, such as craft sticks and construction paper. Have each student cut out his shape, decorate it with a face, and give it an alliterative name. (Trixie Triangle, Oliver Oval, Cecil Circle, and Stareena Star are some examples.) Instead of background scenery, students can create their own background collages. On a large sheet of construction paper, each student will draw and color everyday objects that resemble his shape (and/or cut and paste pictures from old magazines and catalogs). For example, your circle students can make a collage of wheels, the sun, the moon, a globe, coins, and buttons.

During the puppet show, each shape will introduce itself by name, tell about its special features, and explain how it is used every day. The puppet show will be great entertainment (and review) for parents and/or a younger class.

Pattern Fish Crayon Resist Pictures

Literature: *Pattern Fish*, by Trudy Harris

Materials: Heavy paper, crayons, watercolor paint, water, paintbrushes

Activity: Children will learn about patterns with Trudy Harris's book, *Pattern Fish*. Harris uses patterns in her illustrations and borders as well as in the silly story that they accompany. Read the story to your students and see if they can identify the patterns in each illustration. Point out that the author has used the same pattern in the border, the picture, and the text. Then give your students a chance to create pattern fish of their own.

Provide each student with a piece of heavy paper and crayons and ask her to draw a "pattern fish." Explain that, after the pictures of the fish are drawn and colored with crayons, watercolor paint will be used to fill in the ocean. The students will need to press hard with their crayons, so the wax will resist the paint. Remind them that they should illustrate patterns in their fish as well as creating patterned borders. Once the pictures are completed, display them around the room.

Flying Kites

Literature: *Let's Fly a Kite*, by Stuart J. Murphy

Materials: Construction paper, crayons, markers, glue, scissors, ribbons and yarn (optional), fishing line or string, paper clips

Activity: Symmetry is a concept that can help students classify shapes. Examples of symmetry can be found all around us, and students will recognize them easily once they understand the concept. *Let's Fly a Kite*, by Stuart J. Murphy, is a great book to use to introduce symmetry to students. Read the story and discuss the symmetrical shapes as the students identify them throughout the story. Then provide construction paper, crayons, markers, glue, and scissors for the students to use to create their own kites. You could even let them add ribbons or yarn for tails. Once the kites are completed, have the class categorize them into into two groups: symmetrical and not symmetrical. Using fishing line and paper clips, hang the kites from the ceiling to display your students' symmetrical and asymmetrical creations!

Musical Squares

Literature: *Fun with Shapes*, by Peter Patilla

Materials: Unruled index cards, construction paper or butcher paper, markers or crayons, laminator, scissors, cassette tape or CD player and music

Activity: Use this variation of the game Musical Chairs to help students learn to identify different shapes. After reading the book *Fun with Shapes*, by Peter Patilla, to the class, review the shapes the author explores in the book by drawing each on an index card. Then duplicate the shapes on construction paper or butcher paper. These shapes need to be large enough for students to stand on. Laminate the shapes so that they will withstand little feet and you can use them another time. Place the shapes on the floor in a circular path around the perimeter of the room. Make sure there are the same number of shapes as you have students. You may need to make several of each shape—circles, squares, triangles, etc.—since every student must be able to start the game by standing on a shape. Shuffle the index cards and place them in a box or simply hold them facedown.

Begin playing the music and instruct the children to rotate around the shapes until they hear the music stop. When the music stops, the children must stand on the shape that is closest to them. Then, draw an index card from the pile. If you draw a square, every student standing on a square wins that round. Play the game for several rounds as time and interest allow. Alternatively, draw a tally mark on a chart each time a shape is drawn. At the end of the game, count the marks to find out which shape is the winner.

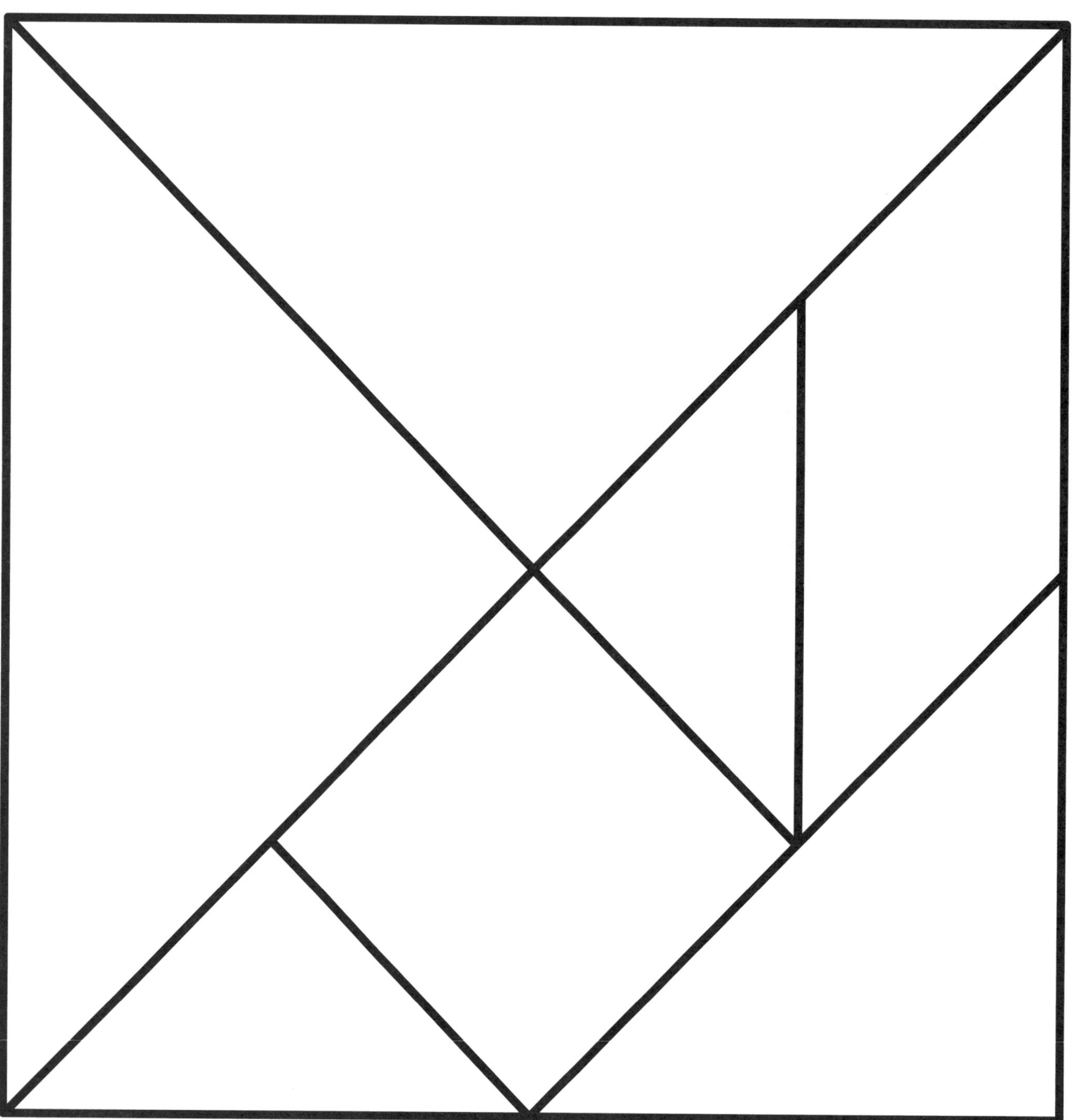

Peanut Butter Clay

Literature: *The Greedy Triangle*, by Marilyn Burns

Materials: 1 c. (237 mL) creamy peanut butter, 1½ c. (356 mL) instant powdered milk, 3 Tbsp. (15 mL) honey, mixing bowl, waxed paper, small decorative candies (candy-coated chocolate pieces, fruit-flavored pieces, hot cinnamon candies, candy corn, etc.)

Activity: Let your students explore shapes and play with their food with this fun edible dough. Mix together the peanut butter, powdered milk, and honey in a mixing bowl until the dough is smooth. If it is too dry, add more honey. If it is too wet, add more powdered milk. (This recipe will make enough dough for 10 small creatures, so you may need to make more than one batch.)

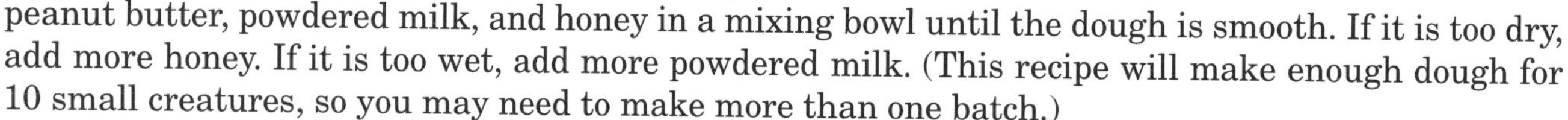

Read *The Greedy Triangle*, by Marilyn Burns. Discuss the shapes that Burns explores in the book. Have students wash their hands before beginning this project. Give each student a portion of the dough and a piece of waxed paper for a work surface, then let her create a shape character like those in the book. Provide small candies for the eyes, nose, and hair. Let the students identify their shapes and perhaps give them names (for example, Tommy the Triangle, Ollie the Octagon, or Samantha the Square). After the children have had a chance to share their creations with the class, let them eat their creatures! *Note:* As with any snack activity, be sure to keep in mind any student allergies. Students who cannot eat peanut butter could use another type of clay for the project.

Clay Solids

Literature: *Cubes, Cones, Cylinders & Spheres*, by Tana Hoban

Materials: Peanut butter clay (recipe above), waxed paper, geometric solids

Activity: Use the recipe above to teach a lesson on solids. Begin by reviewing flat shapes as you introduce the corresponding solid figures one at a time. Hold up an example of each and encourage students to observe the shapes carefully and note the differences and similarities. Also discuss the number of corners, edges, and faces. As you talk about each solid figure, ask your students to name any examples they see in the room. For example: the globe is a sphere, tissue boxes are rectangular prisms, and the trash can may be a cylinder. Next, ask your students to join you on the reading carpet as you show the photographs in *Cubes, Cones, Cylinders & Spheres*, by Tana Hoban. Challenge your students to find as many three-dimensional solids as they can on each page and call them out.

Now that the students have worked up an appetite, it's time to pass out the dough! Give each student a sheet of waxed paper for a work surface and a large chunk of peanut butter clay. Direct students to make a model of each solid figure. After a few minutes, your students should have a row of geometric solids on their desks. Now it's time to dig in and eat their handiwork!

Sugar Cookie Snowpeople

Materials: Sugar cookie dough, resealable plastic bags, waxed paper, decorative candies, spatula, cookie sheets, oven

Activity: Reinforce the concept of circles with these edible snowmen. This is an easy activity with very little preparation if you use commercial cookie dough and divide portions into plastic bags. Give each student a small bag of sugar cookie dough. Let her roll three balls of dough for the snowperson's body. Explain that the top ball should be small, the middle ball a bit bigger, and the bottom ball the largest. After students have made the three dough balls and are happy with the sizes, let them use waxed paper to flatten the balls into circles. Give them sprinkles and other candies to create eyes, a nose, buttons, etc., on their snowpeople. As the students finish decorating their cookies, they can carefully use the spatula to place them on cookie sheets. *Note:* You may want to number the cookie sheets so the children can easily find their own cookies after baking. Consider asking a parent volunteer to help with the baking. Your students will love eating their winter creations!

Shape S'mores

Materials: Waxed paper, graham crackers, large marshmallows, miniature chocolate bars

Activity: Children love sweet snacks! Why not combine a tasty treat with a review of basic shapes? Provide waxed paper on which each student may construct his treat, and remind students to wash their hands before working with food. Give each student one graham cracker broken in half (two squares), one large marshmallow (circle), and a miniature chocolate bar (rectangle). Let them build their delicious treats as you review the basic shapes. For example, you may say, "Select the shape that has four equal sides and four right angles." Each student should place a graham cracker half on the waxed paper. Then tell them to select the shape with no straight lines and place it on the graham cracker. Next, have them select the shape with two sets of equal sides (the rectangle) and so on. When the students finish, let them enjoy their shape s'mores!

At-Home Activities

Quilt Squares

Literature: *The Boy and the Quilt*, by Shirley Kurtz

Materials: Wallpaper, fabric, or wrapping paper squares; card stock; scissors; self-adhesive magnetic strips; butcher paper; backpack; square template from page 54; parent letter from page 55

Activity: Create a class quilt one square at a time. Parents and children will enjoy sharing this activity and contributing to your class masterpiece. Decide how large you want each square to be. Make sure the size of the whole square corresponds with the smaller shapes you cut so that the smaller pieces exactly fit the base square. You may also use the reproducible pattern on page 54. All the base squares need to be the same size, so cut out of card stock or heavy paper more than enough squares for each of the students in your class. Then, cut smaller squares, triangles, and parallelograms out of various wallpaper patterns or wrapping paper. Wallpaper stores may be willing to donate discontinued wallpaper books to your classroom. (Wallpaper is easier for young students to glue, but you can also use fabric squares or wrapping paper.) A parent volunteer might be able to cut out these shapes for you, as you will need a large number and they need to be accurate sizes.

Talk about quilting with your class. Read the story *The Boy and the Quilt*, by Shirley Kurtz, and provide time for the students to examine the illustrations. If you have actual quilts with pattern squares sewn into them, bring them in to share with the students. Then, model the activity with your students. This is easy to do with the whole class if you attach magnetic strips to the back of a number of squares and triangles so that you can arrange them on the board. Then, create your own quilt square to add to a large piece of butcher paper hanging on the wall.

Prepare a backpack that contains the book, the wallpaper pieces, a base square, and a copy of the parent letter. Explain that each student will create one quilt square at home. When he finishes the quilt square, he can bring it back to school and add it to the quilt-in-progress hanging on the wall. You may be amazed at how eager the students will be to add their pieces to the class quilt.

Pasta Lace Ornament

Materials: Pasta in a variety of shapes, bowls, old newspapers or disposable tablecloth, tempera paint, paintbrushes, silver and gold spray paint (optional), ribbon, resealable plastic bags, permanent marker, parent letter (reproducible, page 56)

Activity: Students should enjoy reinforcing shape skills with this holiday activity. Provide different shapes of pasta, such as elbow macaroni, wagon wheels, bow ties, etc. Around the holidays, you may also find special pasta shapes. Before starting this activity, prepare a few examples of pasta ornaments. The ornament can be a free-form shape made with one kind of pasta or a picture framed with pasta shapes. Introduce the activity by showing your ornaments. Encourage the children to plan their ornaments. Provide the pasta in bowls for the children to use. Cover the work area with old newspapers or a disposable tablecloth. Give students different colors of tempera paint and brushes so they can transform the pasta into colorful decorations. (*Note:* You may wish to have an adult volunteer spray paint the pasta with silver and gold paint in a well-ventilated area.) Once the children have painted a variety of pasta shapes and the pasta has dried, let each child select a ribbon she will use to hang her finished ornament. Have the child put all of her pasta shapes and the ribbon into a plastic bag. Use a permanent marker to write the student's name on the bag. Attach a copy of the parent letter to the bag and send the activity home with the student. Parents and their children should enjoy this simple activity that will give them quality time together around the holidays.

Quilt Squares

Quilt Square Base (Use this pattern on card stock or heavy paper.)

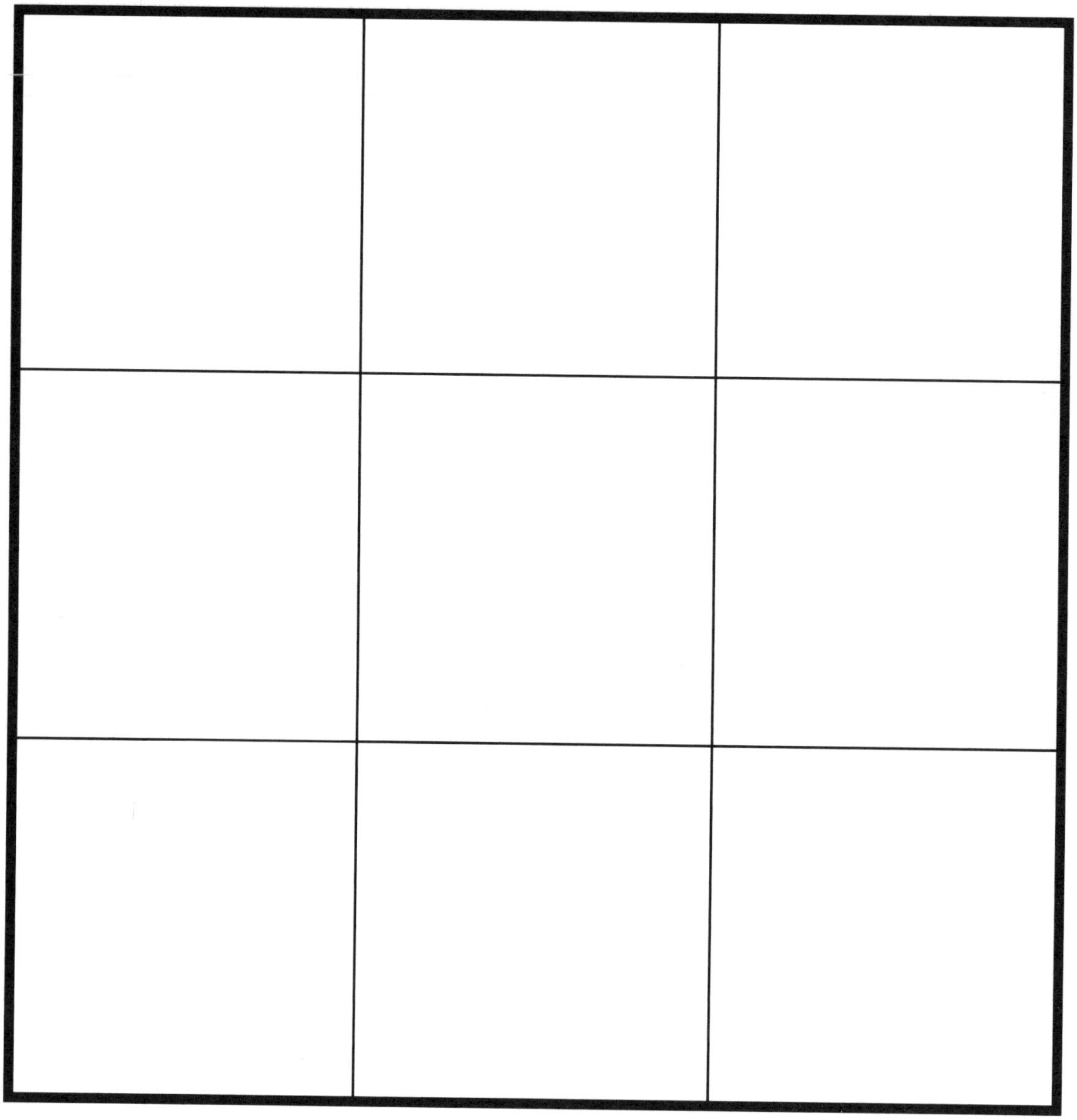

Pattern/Color Shapes (Use this pattern to cut small squares, triangles, and parallelograms out of wallpaper. To make a larger triangular shape, place two small triangles together.)

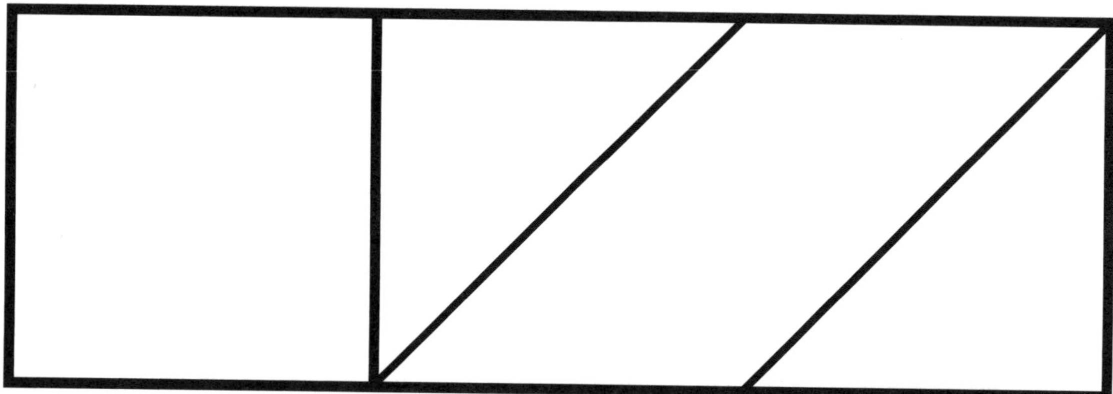

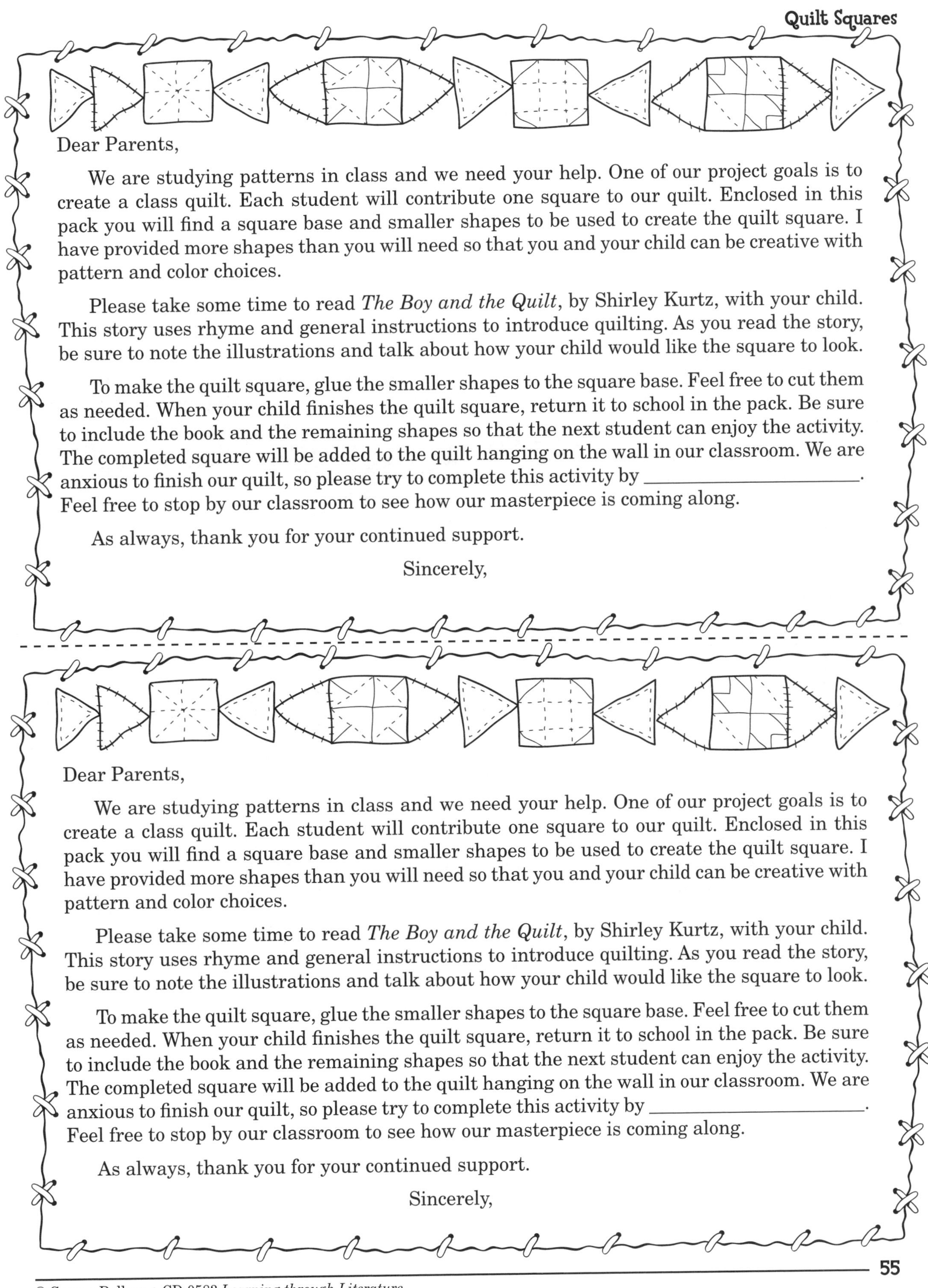

Dear Parents,

We are studying patterns in class and we need your help. One of our project goals is to create a class quilt. Each student will contribute one square to our quilt. Enclosed in this pack you will find a square base and smaller shapes to be used to create the quilt square. I have provided more shapes than you will need so that you and your child can be creative with pattern and color choices.

Please take some time to read *The Boy and the Quilt*, by Shirley Kurtz, with your child. This story uses rhyme and general instructions to introduce quilting. As you read the story, be sure to note the illustrations and talk about how your child would like the square to look.

To make the quilt square, glue the smaller shapes to the square base. Feel free to cut them as needed. When your child finishes the quilt square, return it to school in the pack. Be sure to include the book and the remaining shapes so that the next student can enjoy the activity. The completed square will be added to the quilt hanging on the wall in our classroom. We are anxious to finish our quilt, so please try to complete this activity by ______________________. Feel free to stop by our classroom to see how our masterpiece is coming along.

As always, thank you for your continued support.

Sincerely,

Dear Parents,

We are studying patterns in class and we need your help. One of our project goals is to create a class quilt. Each student will contribute one square to our quilt. Enclosed in this pack you will find a square base and smaller shapes to be used to create the quilt square. I have provided more shapes than you will need so that you and your child can be creative with pattern and color choices.

Please take some time to read *The Boy and the Quilt*, by Shirley Kurtz, with your child. This story uses rhyme and general instructions to introduce quilting. As you read the story, be sure to note the illustrations and talk about how your child would like the square to look.

To make the quilt square, glue the smaller shapes to the square base. Feel free to cut them as needed. When your child finishes the quilt square, return it to school in the pack. Be sure to include the book and the remaining shapes so that the next student can enjoy the activity. The completed square will be added to the quilt hanging on the wall in our classroom. We are anxious to finish our quilt, so please try to complete this activity by ______________________. Feel free to stop by our classroom to see how our masterpiece is coming along.

As always, thank you for your continued support.

Sincerely,

Pasta Lace Ornament

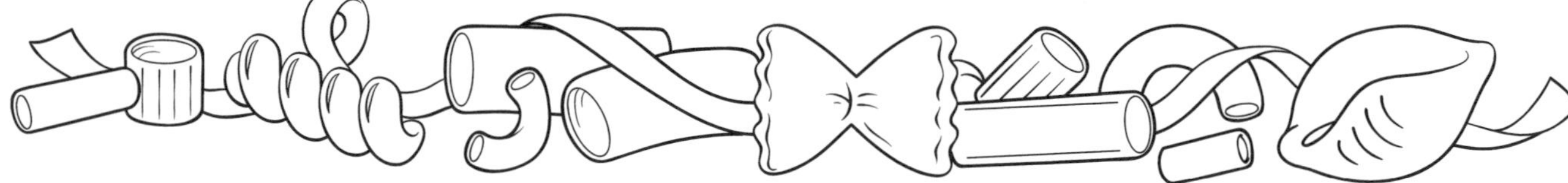

Dear Parents,

The holidays are approaching, and students are brimming with excitement as they share their family traditions and describe the holiday decorations that are transforming their homes. We are studying shapes in class, and your child has painted pasta shapes to prepare for this activity. We have assembled all the materials you will need to create a beautiful ornament together. Take some time to work with your child and arrange the shapes into a pasta lace ornament. Using a sheet of waxed paper as a work surface, glue the pasta pieces together to make a flat shape. Your child may decide to leave a space in the middle of the ornament to add a family photo. Once the ornament is dry, attach the ribbon so that you can hang the ornament in your home. Be sure to write the date on the ornament so that years from now you can look back with fond memories at this time shared with your child.

Once again, thank you for your continued involvement in your child's education. It makes a world of difference!

Sincerely,

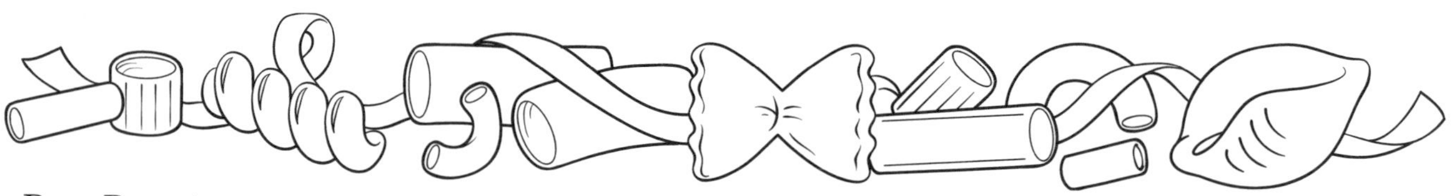

Dear Parents,

The holidays are approaching, and students are brimming with excitement as they share their family traditions and describe the holiday decorations that are transforming their homes. We are studying shapes in class, and your child has painted pasta shapes to prepare for this activity. We have assembled all the materials you will need to create a beautiful ornament together. Take some time to work with your child and arrange the shapes into a pasta lace ornament. Using a sheet of waxed paper as a work surface, glue the pasta pieces together to make a flat shape. Your child may decide to leave a space in the middle of the ornament to add a family photo. Once the ornament is dry, attach the ribbon so that you can hang the ornament in your home. Be sure to write the date on the ornament so that years from now you can look back with fond memories at this time shared with your child.

Once again, thank you for your continued involvement in your child's education. It makes a world of difference!

Sincerely,

Number Facts

Students need lots of practice in basic number facts, and these activities will make that experience fun and memorable!

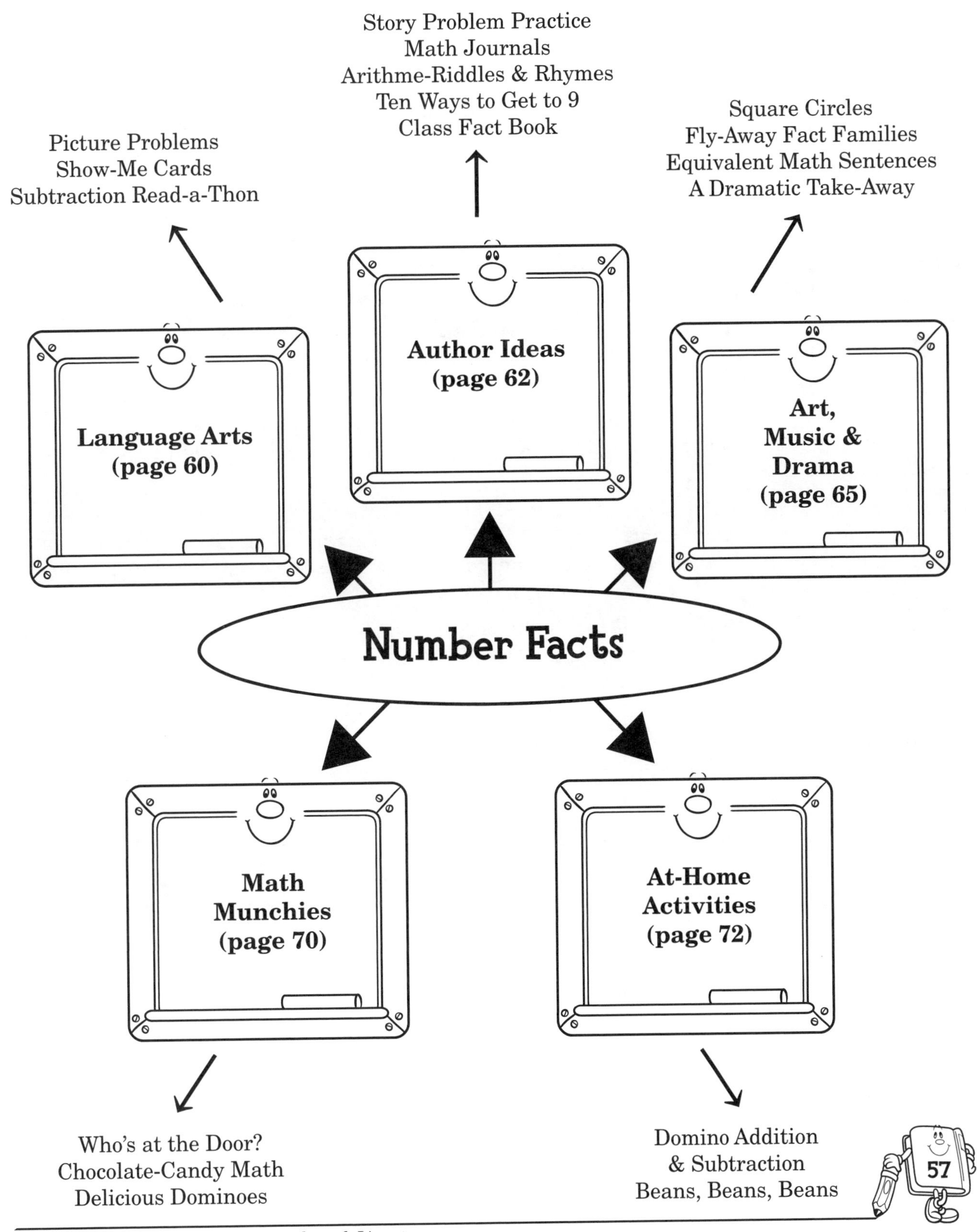

Featured Literature

The following selections are used in conjunction with the activities in this section. You may want to obtain them from your library before you start the unit. (Activities with which the books are used are listed in parentheses.)

12 Ways to Get 11, by Eve Merriam (Simon & Schuster Books for Young Readers, 1993). This book uses big, bold illustrations and simple text to illustrate number sets that equal eleven. This is a great resource to use with large group readings. (Math Journals, page 62; Ten Ways to Get 9, page 64)

Arithme-Tickle: An Even Number of Odd Riddle-Rhymes, by J. Patrick Lewis (Harcourt, Inc., 2002). Rhyme, illustrations, and riddles are used to present 18 math word problems. This is a great book to share with children who dread story problems. (Arithme-Riddles & Rhymes, page 64)

Domino Addition, by Lynette Long (Charlesbridge, 1996). This book provides an introduction to addition through the use of dominoes. (Delicious Dominoes, page 71; Domino Addition & Subraction, page 72)

The Doorbell Rang, by Pat Hutchins (Greenwillow Books, 1986). Explore basic math operations with this story about children and cookies. The story begins with two children and a big plate of cookies. Each time the doorbell rings, more children arrive to share the cookies. (Who's at the Door? page 70)

The Grapes of Math: Mind Stretching Math Riddles, by Greg Tang (Scholastic, 2001). Easy text and bold colorful illustrations are used in this book that explores number sets and beginning multiplication skills. (Class Fact Book, page 64)

The Great Take-Away, by Louise Mathews (Dodd, Mead, 1980). Students are introduced to subtraction and story problems in this charming tale of a lazy hog who takes from others rather than working himself. (A Dramatic Take-Away, page 66)

Jack and the Beanstalk, retold and illustrated by Steven Kellogg (Morrow Junior Books, 1991). Kellogg retells the traditional tale of Jack and the Beanstalk. (Beans, Beans, Beans, page 72)

Math for All Seasons, by Greg Tang (Scholastic Press, 2002). Each page in this beautiful book includes a riddle with clues for determining the solutions. Children are encouraged to try strategies other than rote counting. (Show-Me Cards, page 60; Class Fact Book, page 64)

Mission: Addition, by Loreen Leedy (Holiday House, 1997). Leedy uses several short tales to explore vocabulary and the process of addition. Colorful illustrations, simple explanations, and addition problems help students clarify signs, sums, regrouping, and checking their work. This is a great book to use either as an introduction of basic addition or as a review. (Picture Problems, page 60)

More M&M's Brand Chocolate Candies Math, by Barbara Barbieri McGrath (Charlesbridge, 1998). McGrath uses M&M's® to introduce beginning multiplication, division, and graphing. (Chocolate-Candy Math, page 71)

My Full Moon Is Square, by Elinor J. Pinczes (Houghton Mifflin Company, 2002). The author uses fireflies to demonstrate number sets in this charming book about a frog who needs more light to read when the clouds block the moonlight. (Square Circles, page 65)

Number One Number Fun, by Kay Chorao (Holiday House, 1995). A variety of addition and subtraction problems are presented in a lively verse as an animal circus performs. (Equivalent Math Sentences, page 66)

The Shark Swimathon, by Stuart J. Murphy (HarperCollins, 2001). Readers will get plenty of practice subtracting with regrouping in this tale of a shark swim team working together to reach a goal. (Subtraction Read-a-Thon, page 61)

Subtraction Action, by Loreen Leedy (Holiday House, 2000). Miss Prime leads her class of creatures through several subtraction lessons. Important vocabulary and skills, such as missing addends and regrouping, are covered. (Story Problem Practice, page 62)

Additional Suggested Literature

Anno's Magic Seeds, by Mitsumasa Anno (Philomel Books, 1995). Jack is given two seeds that will produce two fruits and two seeds. He plants two seeds, which in turn harvest four fruits. He then plants three seeds and so on. Older students will enjoy the challenge of figuring the new total of fruit before you turn the page.

The Hershey's Kisses Addition Book, by Jerry Pallotta (Scholastic, 2001). Children will love practicing their addition with this easy to read and follow book. Pallotta uses Hershey's Kisses® candies as manipulatives to work through basic addition facts.

One Less Fish, by Kim Michelle Toft and Allan Sheather (Charlesbridge, 1998). This cautionary tale takes place in the Great Barrier Reef and illustrates through simple subtraction what might have happened to the sea creatures if they were not protected by law. Subtext explores the many dangers to this fragile ecosystem.

There Were Ten in the Bed (Weldon Kids Pty., Ltd., 1997). Colorful illustrations, unique animals, and fun repetition demonstrate the concept of subtracting one in this story. Facts about each animal species are also provided at the end of the book.

Picture Problems

Literature: *Mission: Addition*, by Loreen Leedy

Materials: Construction paper, crayons or markers

Activity: After reading Loreen Leedy's book *Mission: Addition* to your class, give students an opportunity to demonstrate what they know about adding numbers. One of the tales in this book describes inventing word problems with pictures. Share the picture problems in the book and brainstorm some other ideas for picture problems. Then provide students with large pieces of construction paper and crayons or markers. Let them create picture problems to share with the class. More advanced students may even want to write the story problems on the back of their posters. When students have finished, let them take turns holding up their pictures to share with the class. Then display the picture problems around the room.

Show-Me Cards

Literature: *Math for All Seasons*, by Greg Tang

Materials: Index cards, crayons or markers, resealable plastic bags or rubber bands

Activity: This class activity can be used to practice basic facts in addition or subtraction. Provide each student with 10 index cards. Instruct them to write the numerals 0–9, one on each card, in large bold print. Then, as you walk around the room, give your students two addends and ask them to hold up the card with the correct sum. This is a great activity to involve everyone and reinforce basic math facts.

Share the book *Math for All Seasons*, by Greg Tang, with the students. As you read each riddle, ask the students to demonstrate their understanding of the basic facts by holding up the appropriate card. In this way the students in the class who may need additional reinforcement can be quickly identified. Students can store their Show-Me Cards in resealable plastic bags, or you can give each student a rubber band to wrap around the cards.

Extension: Extend the Show-Me game described above by using it for place value practice. Each child should have 10 Show-Me cards faceup on his desk. Call out both extended numbers and standard numbers. Your students will demonstrate their knowledge of place value by assembling digits in the correct order on their desks with the Show-Me cards. As you circulate around the room, it will be easy for you to see which students understand place value and those who may need more practice.

Subtraction Read-a-Thon

Literature: *The Shark Swimathon*, by Stuart J. Murphy

Materials: Poster board, marker

Activity: Your students will get plenty of subtraction practice when you read about a shark swim team's swimming goal in *The Shark Swimathon*, by Stuart J. Murphy. The book uses large numbers to provide reinforcement with regrouping, but as you complete this activity, the numbers you choose can be as big or small as your mathematicians' abilities allow. In the story, the sharks begin with a large number for a goal and subtract smaller numbers as they work toward that goal. Your class can do the same by setting a weekly reading goal. Determine the number of books you want to read aloud in a week, 20, for example. Write the number 20 on a piece of poster board. Keep a tally of the books you read aloud each day. At the close of each day, subtract the day's tally from your goal. Monday, your poster could read 20 – 3 = 17, Tuesday, 17 – 4 = 13, and so on throughout the week. You may set higher goals as your students' experience with subtraction increases. Each day your students will see real world subtraction in action, as well as be exposed to all that great literature!

Extension: As the class completes its reading goals for each week, ask your students to record their progress on a pictograph. Provide construction paper cutouts in the shape of books, to which students can add the title and author of each book you have read. Create a graph on chart paper entitled "Our Weekly Reading Goal." Label the vertical axis with the number of books and the horizontal axis with the day of the week. Students can attach the paper cutouts to record the books the class reads aloud. As you add the books you have read each day, give the students an opportunity to practice writing number sentences that reflect the additions to the graph.

Author Ideas

Story Problem Practice

Literature: *Subtraction Action*, by Loreen Leedy

Materials: Consumable manipulatives (such as buttons or popcorn kernels), construction paper, glue, pencils

Activity: Story problems become no problem at all when you read *Subtraction Action*, by Loreen Leedy. Miss Prime is back, this time to teach her class about subtraction. Let Miss Prime teach your class, too, with the help of consumable manipulatives like buttons or popcorn kernels and a construction paper mat on which to work. As you read the story, have the students move around their tokens to assemble the problems at their desk. Finish the lesson by sharing the characters' Subtraction Stories on the copyright page. Use these as a springboard for creating your own. Direct each student to make up a word problem in her head. Then, she should write the basic fact from the problem on the construction paper and glue the manipulatives to the paper to represent the fact. Take turns sharing the word problems aloud. As each student shares her problem, encourage her peers to solve it. The student can then show her project to confirm the correct answer.

Math Journals

Literature: *12 Ways to Get 11*, by Eve Merriam

Materials: Beans or other small counters, paper cups, Adding Up! sheet (reproducible, page 63), paper, construction paper, stapler, crayons, pencils

Activity: As shown in the beautiful book *12 Ways to Get 11*, there are often many problems with the same solution. With a handful of beans and a cup, students can practice addition facts with a common sum. Give students 12 counters (e.g., dry beans or base ten blocks), a cup, and a copy of page 63. Have students shake out the beans onto their papers. Some will land on each side of the paper. Each side's number of beans will become an addend in a math sentence where the sum is always 12. Students should write each fact they discover at the bottom of their papers. Allow them to continue rolling out the counters and making new number sentences for about five minutes. Share and compare the resulting facts.

At the conclusion of the lesson, students can keep track of all the ways to make 12 in a math journal. Staple several sheets of paper together using construction paper for the journal's cover. Students can illustrate the facts with crayons, then write the addends and resulting sums as number sentences.

Extension: When the class is sharing all the facts they found, take the opportunity to teach the properties of addition. An example of the identity, or zero property, is 12 + 0 = 12. The commutative property is demonstrated with 7 + 5 and 5 + 7.

Name:____________________________ Date:________________

Adding Up!

Directions: Gently spill your math counters out on the paper. Use the counters on each side of the box to make up a math fact. Write each fact below.

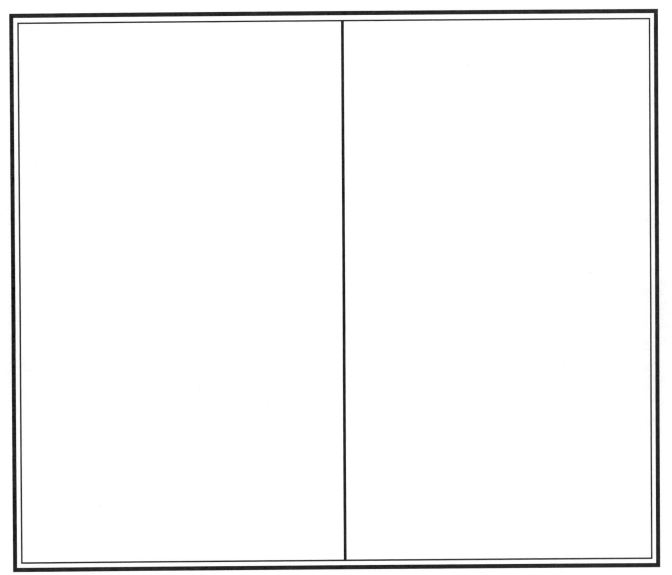

Addition Facts:

Arithme-Riddles & Rhymes

Literature: *Arithme-Tickle: An Even Number of Odd Riddle-Rhymes* by J. Patrick Lewis

Materials: Paper and pencils

Activity: Let students create story problems in the form of fun riddles and rhymes while reinforcing basic math facts. Share the book *Arithme-Tickle*, by Frank Remkiewicz, with the class. This book contains 18 word problems disguised as rhyming riddles. Read a few of the riddles together and give the class an opportunity to solve them. Then, divide the class into smaller groups and give each group of students one riddle to solve collaboratively and report later about the process they used.

Next, explain to the groups that they will write their own rhyming riddles to share with the class. Tell them to first decide on a word problem and then use creative language to rewrite it as a rhyming riddle. When all the groups have finished, collect the riddles and use a word processor to publish your own class "Arithme-Riddle" book.

Ten Ways to Get 9

Literature: *12 Ways to Get 11*, by Eve Merriam

Materials: Materials to make class books

Activity: In *12 Ways to Get 11*, by Eve Merriam, the art on each page depicts the sum of 11. A natural springboard for this storybook is to have your students create their own. Your class can publish "Ten Ways to Get 9," "Thirteen Ways to Get 12," "Eleven Ways to Get 10," etc. If you choose to use more than two addends or include subtraction facts, the number of possible combinations increases.

Class Fact Book

Literature: *The Grapes of Math: Mind Stretching Math Riddles*, by Gregory Tang; *Math for All Seasons*, by Gregory Tang

Materials: Computer with simple drawing software, printer, and paper

Activity: Students can create a class fact book by drawing or stamping two or three groups of objects that represent addends. Some students may enjoy creating story problems like the ones in *Math for All Seasons*, by Gregory Tang. Each page of this book offers a riddle that can be solved using simple math techniques. Students may enjoy trying to solve one or two of the riddles at the beginning of each math class. With some assistance, students can type similar simple word problems, then use the software to illustrate the calculations.

Square Circles

Literature: *My Full Moon Is Square*, by Elinor Pinczes

Materials: Firefly pattern (reproducible, page 67), tagboard or heavy paper, scissors, laminator (optional), masking tape or self-adhesive magnetic strips, paper, stamps and stamp pads or stamping markers, pencils or crayons, construction paper

Activity: Explore number sets and practice beginning multiplication skills with the picture book, *My Full Moon Is Square*, by Elinor Pinczes. Use the firefly reproducible on page 67 to create a set of board manipulatives to use with this activity. Make several copies of this page on tagboard and cut out each firefly. You may want to laminate them for durability. Then use masking tape on the back of each or attach small magnetic strips so the manipulatives can be rearranged easily on the chalkboard.

Read the book aloud to the class. Each time the fireflies create a new square number set, choose a student to go to the board and arrange the manipulatives to match the illustration. See if the students can also write the number sentence that corresponds with each number set. (For example, four rows of four fireflies would be 4 x 4.)

Next, give each student a piece of drawing paper and provide stamps or stamp markers. Ask students to draw a scene they remember from the book using the stamps to create the firefly number set. Mount the drawings on colorful construction paper and hang them on a bulletin board. You could add a string of blinking decorative lights around the perimeter of the bulletin board to look like fireflies. Use construction paper to make leaves and tall grasses to cover the light cord.

Fly-Away Fact Families

Materials: Butterfly pattern (reproducible, page 68), construction paper, pencils, crayons or markers

Activity: Introduce related addition and subtraction facts as a fact family. Each family has four facts: two addition and two subtraction. Remind your young learners that, when subtracting, the largest number goes first. Provide each student with a copy of the butterfly pattern and a sheet of contruction paper. First, fold the paper in half. Then guide students through the process of tracing the shape on the paper to cut out a symmetrical butterfly with four wings. Students can write one fact from the fact family on each wing and then color or decorate the butterfly.

Equivalent Math Sentences

Literature: *Number One Number Fun*, by Kay Chorao

Materials: Chart paper and marker, circus tent pattern (reproducible, page 69), pencils, crayons and/or markers

Activity: Share the book *Number One Number Fun*, by Kay Chorao, with your students. They will enjoy practicing the basic facts with this story about circus feats. Gather the children in a group, near the chalkboard or with chart paper handy. As you read each page, call on student volunteers to solve the problems on the board. Your students may notice that many of the problems have the same answer. Develop this line of thinking by writing one number on the board, such as 9. Now, think aloud as you write several addition and subtraction number combinations that are all equal to 9, for example: 3 + 3 + 3, 4 + 5, 2 + 4 + 3, 11 – 2, and 18 – 9.

Next, give each student a copy of the reproducible on page 69. Assign one number to each student to write on the top of his tent. Then, on the sides of the tent, he should write several combinations of numbers that equal the given number. Let students color and decorate the tents. Hang the finished products on a bulletin board titled "Under the Big Top!"

A Dramatic Take-Away

Literature: *The Great Take-Away*, by Louise Mathews

Activity: Read the book *The Great Take-Away*, by Louise Mathews. Your students will enjoy solving the subtraction mysteries presented in this book. Emphasize the moral at the end of the book, which reminds students that stealing is wrong. Explain that the class will practice subtraction skills as they dramatize the story. To do this, students will take turns portraying the main character from the story. As a class, decide upon the name of the superhero (Minus Man, Math Magician, etc.).

The first day, designate a student to help you hide a prominent classroom item. The second day, a different student will help you hide two classroom items. Each day, the rest of the class will try to identify the missing items. The student who identifies the item(s) first is the superhero. When each missing object has been discovered, write the phrase from the book on the board. ("There are ______ (number) ___________(item). ________(number) are left. How many were taken away in the theft?") Fill in the blanks with the appropriate numbers and words to reinforce the concept of subtraction each day. Continue with the activity until every student has had the opportunity to help you hide an item.

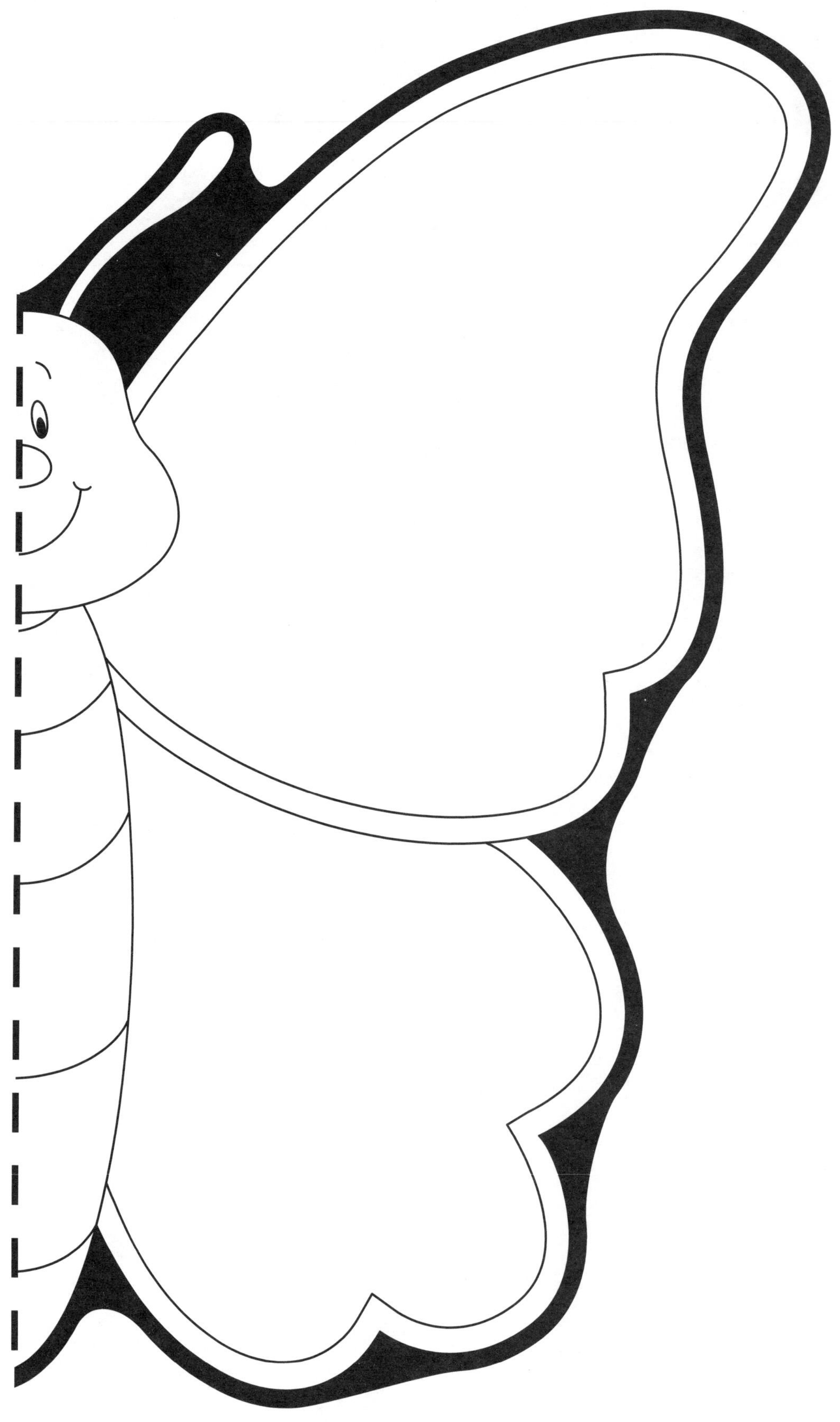

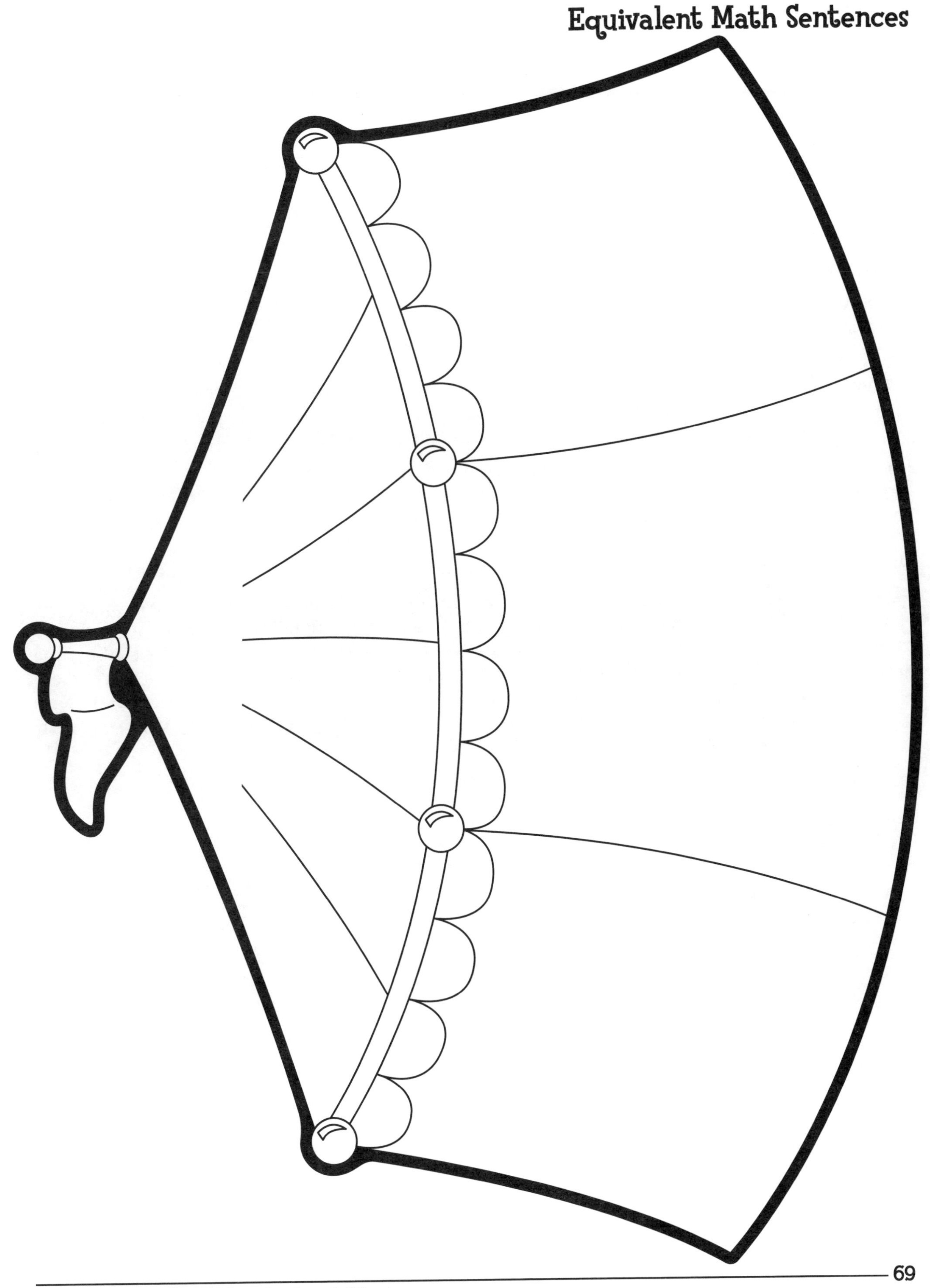

Math Munchies

Who's at the Door?

Literature: *The Doorbell Rang*, by Pat Hutchins

Materials: Cookies (enough for each student to have one), chart paper and marker or chalkboard and chalk

Activity: Pat Hutchins's story, *The Doorbell Rang*, is about two children who start with a huge plate of homemade cookies that are "just like Grandma's." Each time the doorbell rings, more children arrive to share the cookies and each child's pile of cookies gets smaller and smaller. Your students will enjoy acting out a variation of this story to illustrate the concept of subtraction.

Prepare a plate of cookies that has one for each student in your class. Select two students to sit at a large table and each take a cookie from the plate. Ask another student to keep track of the subtraction process on the chalkboard or chart paper. Have that student write down the number of cookies with which you began and then, as a class, subtract two for the students at the table. (Example: We started with 25 cookies and two children each took one, so our subtraction problem will be 25 – 2 = 23.)

Select one student to be the "knocker." Instruct the "knocker" to stand by the door and knock on your signal. As you silently walk around the room, tap the number of students that you want to join the two children at the table. Each time students join the table and each takes a cookie, pause the game long enough to talk about the subtraction process that was just demonstrated. (Example: Three more students joined the table and took a cookie, so now our subtraction problem is 23 – 3 = 20.) Make sure that your "knocker" and the recorder at the board get their cookies, too. Then enjoy the tasty treat!

Chocolate-Candy Math

Literature: *More M&M's Brand Chocolate Candies Math*, by Barbara Barbieri McGrath

Materials: Candy-coated chocolate pieces

Activity: Barbara Barbieri McGrath has written an addition book using M&M's® brand candies for manipulatives, titled *More M&M's Brand Chocolate Candies Math*. Children can practice counting, adding, sorting, and graphing candies with the activities in this book. Provide each student with a small bag of candies. As you read the book to the students, walk around the room to monitor student work as well as give struggling students an opportunity to see the clear illustrations.

Once you have completed the activities in the book, you can include other addition and subtraction activities of your own. For example, tell the students to add the blue candies to the red candies to find a sum. You may ask the students to count their green candies, then eat two of them and tell how many they have left. For a class challenge activity, ask the students to count their candies and write their totals on the board. Then ask the students to see if they can figure out how many candies the class has altogether. When you have finished adding and subtracting, the students will be anxious to eat their treats!

Delicious Dominoes

Literature: *Domino Addition*, by Lynette Long

Materials: Graham crackers, miniature marshmallows, prepared chocolate frosting, paper and pencils

Activity: Use the counting book *Domino Addition*, by Lynette Long, as a springboard for a tasty addition treat. You will need graham crackers, miniature marshmallows, and a can of icing. Create dominoes by spreading a thin layer of icing on each graham cracker and then adding mini marshmallows to represent the dots. Using each half of her edible domino as an addend, have each student write down the resulting math fact on a piece of paper. Each student should then leave her domino on her desk. Taking their papers with them, students can move from desk to desk, round-robin style, and record the new domino addends. When the students return to their seats, they can find the sums while munching on their own dominoes.

At-Home Activities

Domino Addition & Subtraction

Literature: *Domino Addition*, by Lynette Long

Materials: Dominoes, parent letter (reproducible, page 73), activity sheets (reproducibles, pages 74 and 75), backpack or tote bag

Activity: *Domino Addition*, by Lynette Long, provides a visual introduction to addition facts. Using each side of a domino as an addend, the book illustrates calculating a sum by counting the dots. Take this concept one step further by sending home the book and a set of dominoes, along with a copy of page 74. After reading the book with family members, the student should spread the dominoes facedown on a table. He can then turn over two dominoes to reveal a math problem. Finally, he should replicate the domino dots on his copy of page 74, write the addends, and solve the math problems.

Dominoes can also provide subtraction practice. Page 75 has a recording sheet for subtraction problems. Children and parents will use the two halves of each domino to create the problems to solve. Your students should agree that using dominoes to practice facts really adds up! (If you choose to do only addition, you will need to reword the parent letter.)

Beans, Beans, Beans

Literature: *Jack and the Beanstalk*, retold and illustrated by Steven Kellogg

Materials: Backpack, copy of *Jack and the Beanstalk*, parent letter (reproducible, page 73), resealable plastic bag, dry lima beans or pinto beans, activity sheet (reproducible, page 76)

Activity: Many parents want to help their children with basic fact practice, but are not sure how. This simple activity reinforces both shared reading and basic addition and subtraction using beans as manipulatives.

Prepare a backpack that includes the book *Jack and the Beanstalk*, a copy of the parent letter on page 73, and a resealable plastic bag of uncooked lima beans or pinto beans. Send the pack home with a student. Encourage parents to read the book with their children and use the beans as manipulatives to practice basic addition and subtraction. Let families keep the beans for continued practice after they have returned the backpack to school. Then simply add another bag of beans to the pack and give it to another child to take home.

    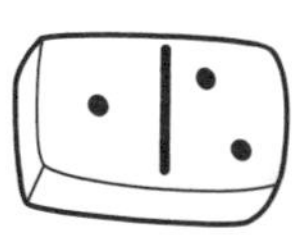  

Dear Parents,

We are practicing addition and subtraction facts in class, and we know that reading books and playing with dominoes adds up to pure fun! Using the dots on the dominoes to add and subtract is a fresh way of reinforcing the basic facts and a satisfying change from flashcards. Begin by reading *Domino Addition* with your child. After you have practiced the math presented in the book, it's time for the fun to begin!

Dump out the container of dominoes. They need to be facedown for addition and faceup for subtraction. As you complete the worksheets, encourage your child to count the dots as needed for support.

Please return the storybook, dominoes, and completed worksheets by ______________________.

Thank you. Your support plus your cooperation equals a more constructive learning environment.

Sincerely,

Beans, Beans, Beans

Dear Parents,

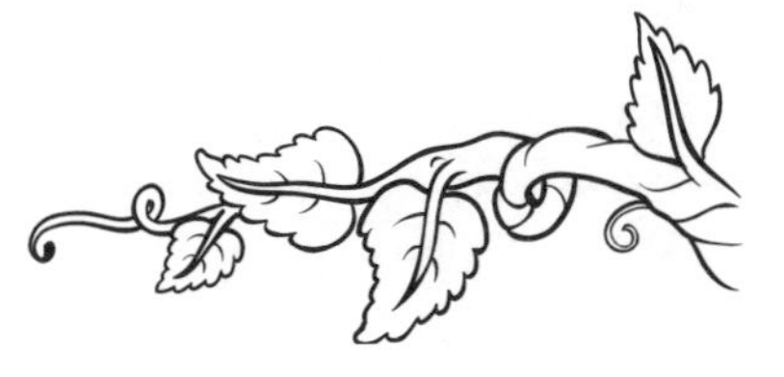

We are really working hard to learn all of our basic addition and subtraction facts up to 12. Please take a few moments to sit down with your child and enjoy the enclosed book, *Jack and the Beanstalk*, by Steven Kellogg. After you have read the book together, use the beans to practice basic facts with your child. For example, ask your child to "show me 3 beans plus 4 beans" and the answer. Have your child record the math problem on the worksheet. Take turns using the beans as manipulatives to illustrate problems and let your child quiz you. This modeling can be valuable instruction as well.

When you are finished with the book, please return it to school in the backpack so that another family can enjoy it. Keep the bag of beans to continue practicing basic facts at home. Here are some other ways you can practice facts with your child:

- Make up simple word problems at dinnertime. For example, "We had 7 pieces of chicken. Each of us ate 1 piece. How many do we have left?"
- On the way to extracurricular activities, use your child's interests to practice basic facts. For example, while driving to your child's soccer game, quiz him or her with problems like, "Our team scored 3 goals in Friday's game and 5 goals in Saturday's game. How many goals did we score in all?"

Thank you for your continued support.

Sincerely,

Name:______________________________ Date:________________

Domino Addition

Directions: Choose two real dominoes. Draw the dots on the paper. Add and record the fact. Continue to fill in all the pictures with different facts.

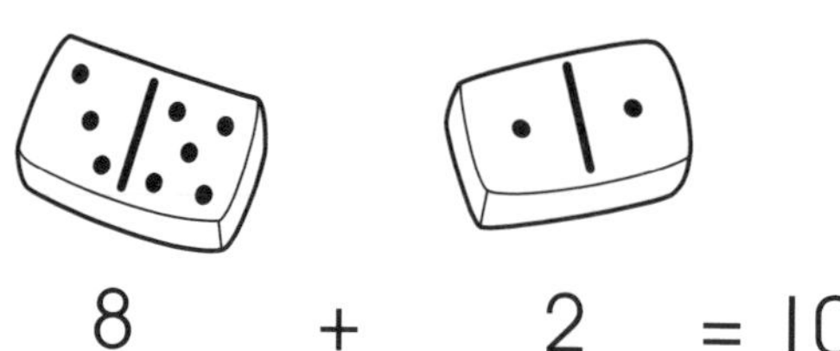

8 + 2 = 10

+

____ + ____ = ____

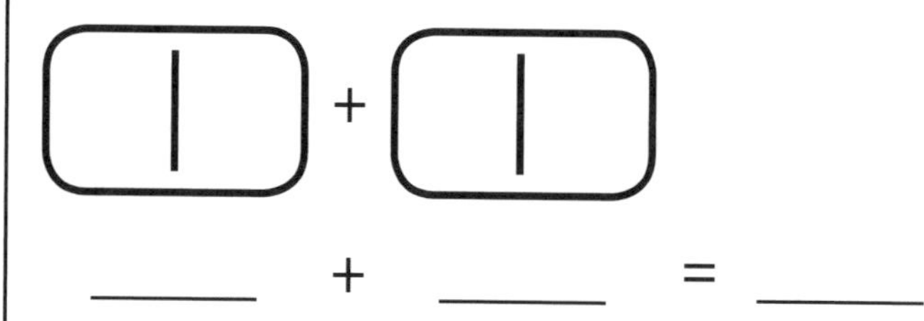

____ + ____ = ____

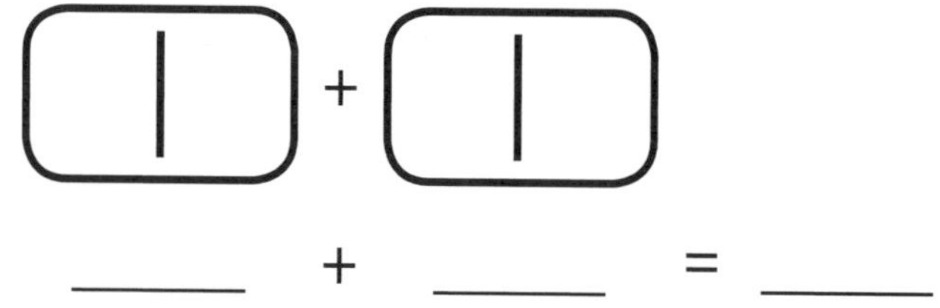

____ + ____ = ____

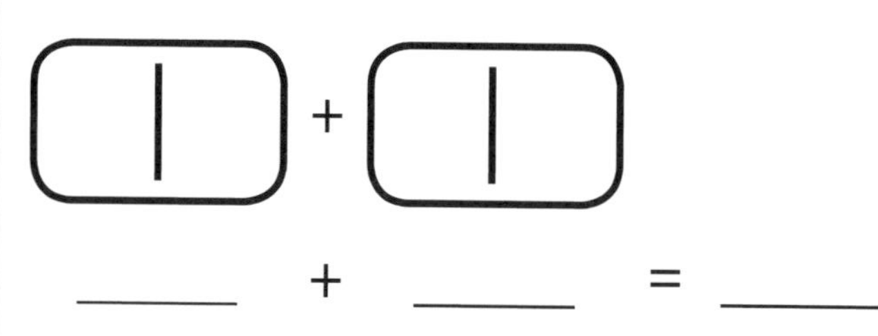

____ + ____ = ____

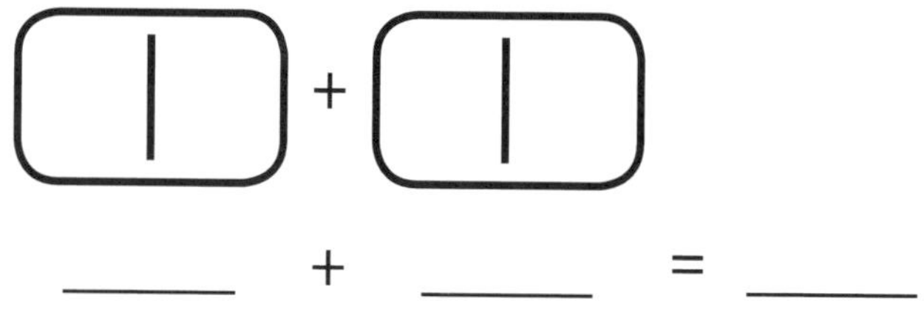

____ + ____ = ____

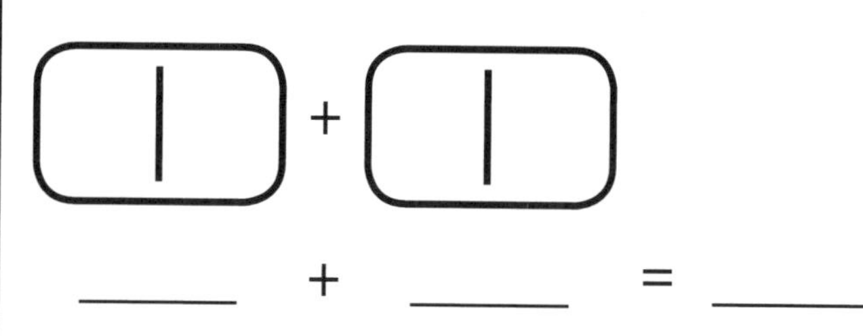

____ + ____ = ____

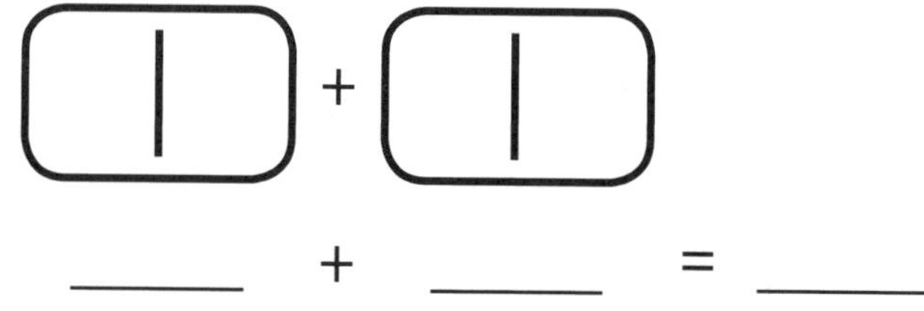

____ + ____ = ____

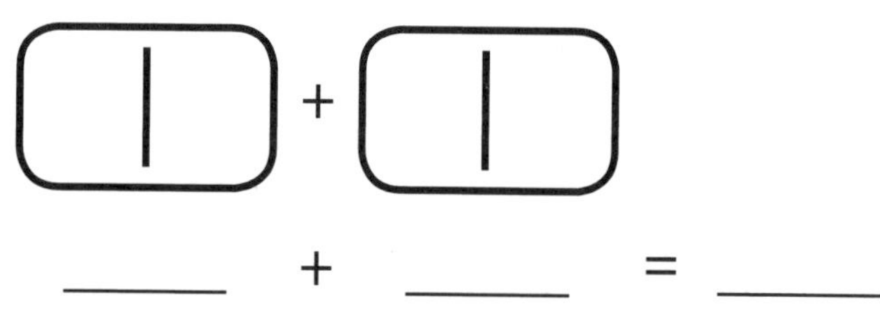

____ + ____ = ____

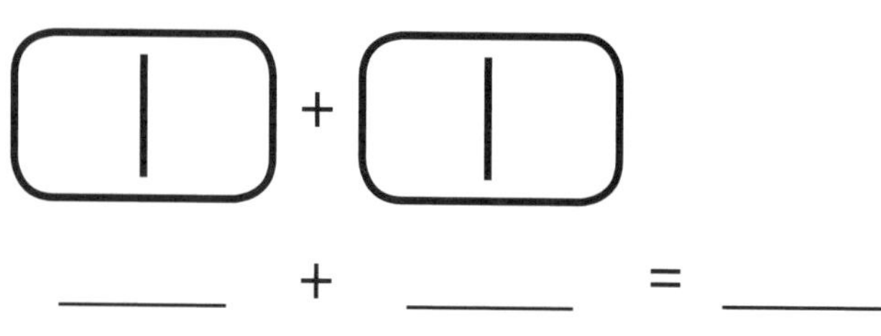

____ + ____ = ____

+

____ + ____ = ____

Name:______________________________ Date:________________

Domino Subtraction

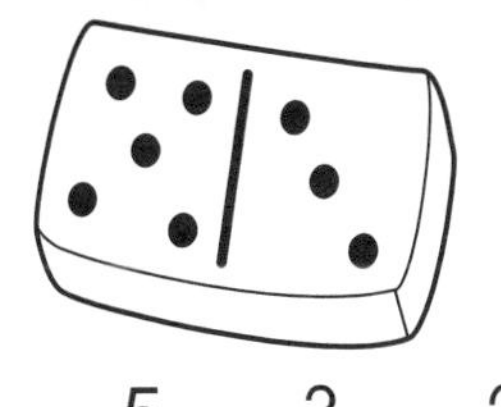
5 – 3 = 2

Directions: Arrange all the dominoes faceup in front of you. Look at the dots on each domino and subtract.

Find the dominoes that match the **difference** shown in each row. Draw the dots.

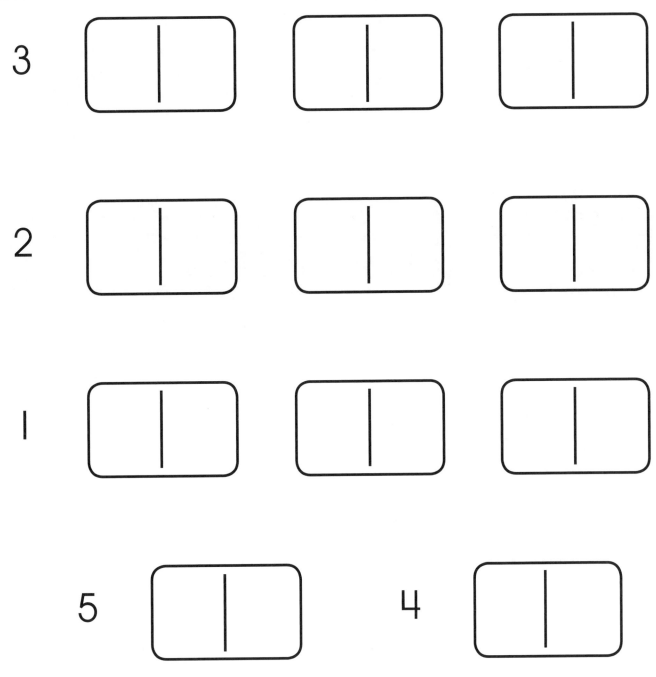

3   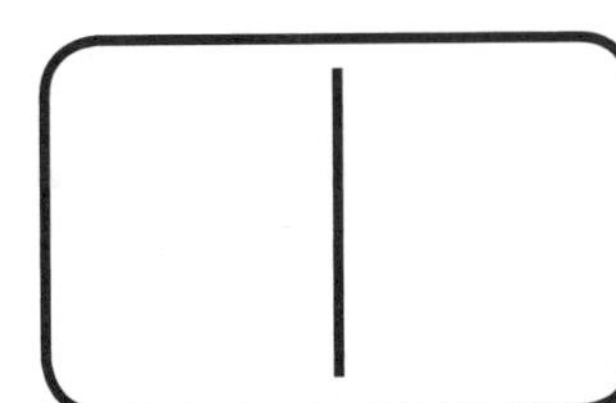

2 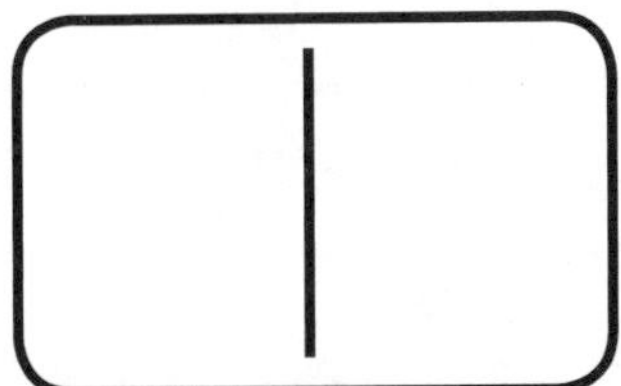 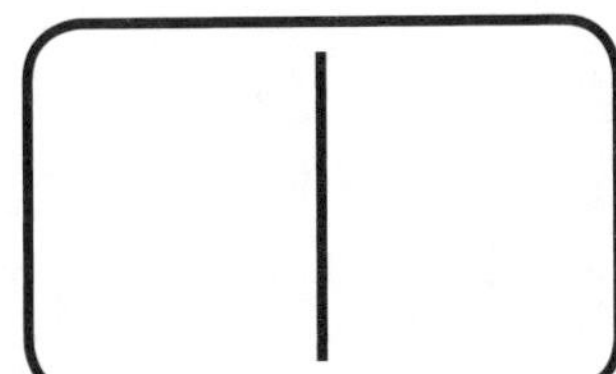 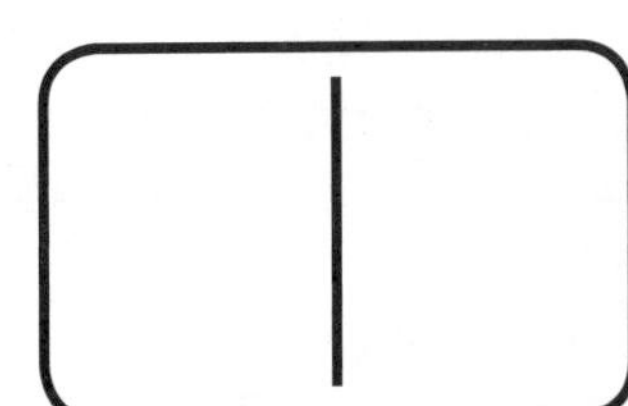

1 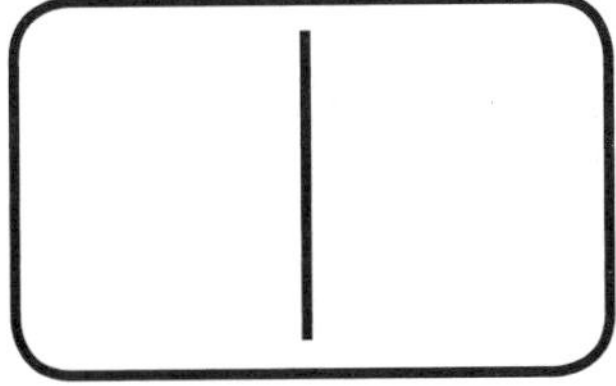 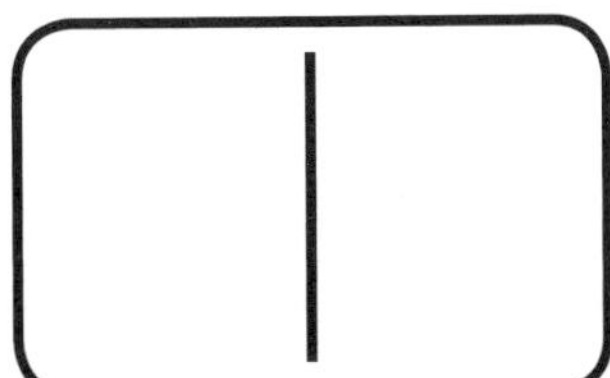 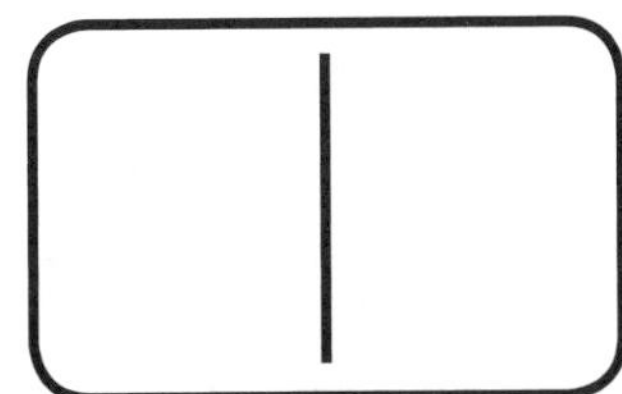

5 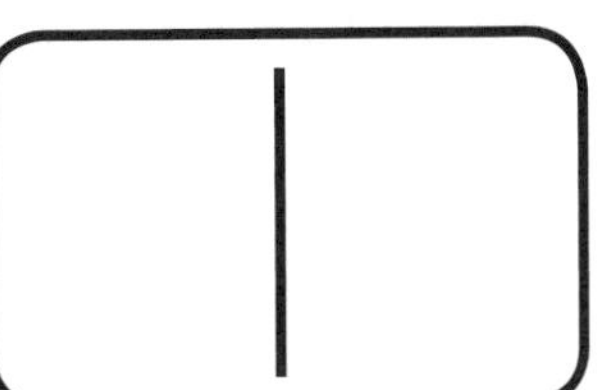 4 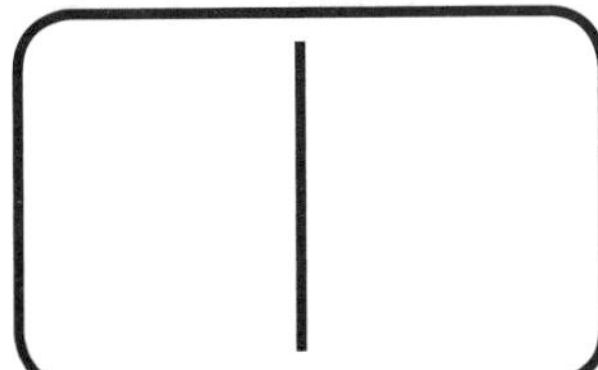

Name:_______________________________ Date:_______________

Beans, Beans, Beans

Directions: Write a math fact in the blanks. Use the beans to find the sum. Draw the beans in the boxes.

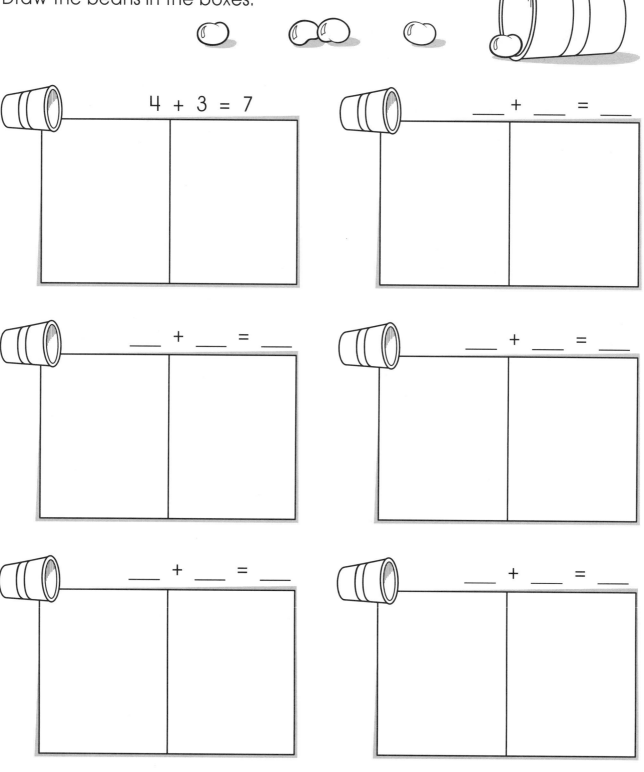

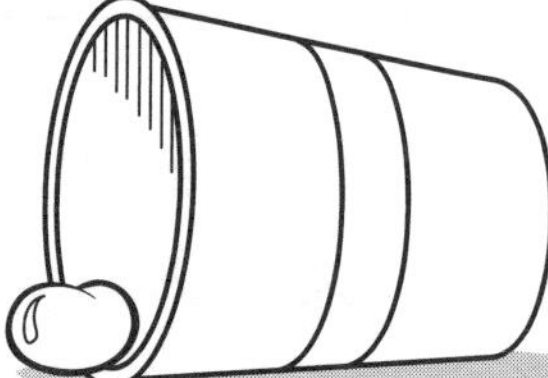

4 + 3 = 7

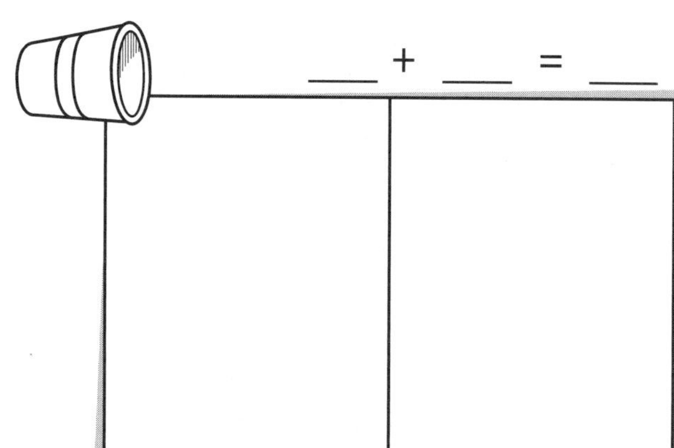

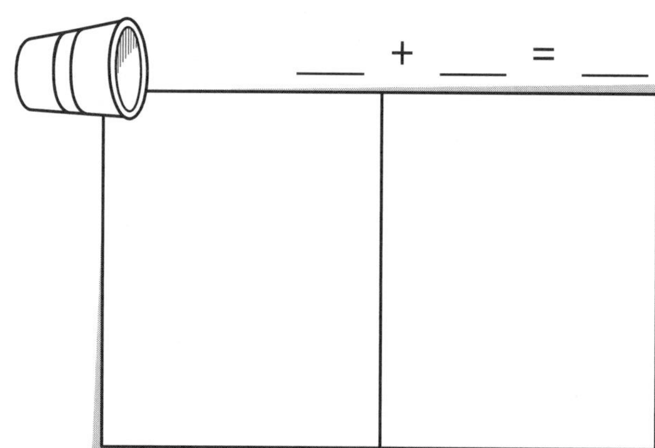

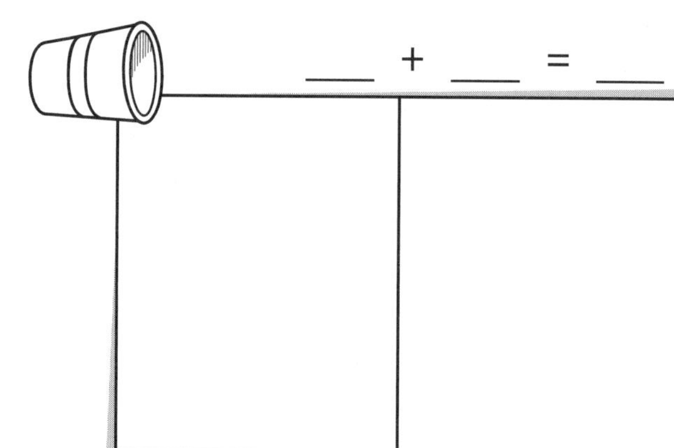

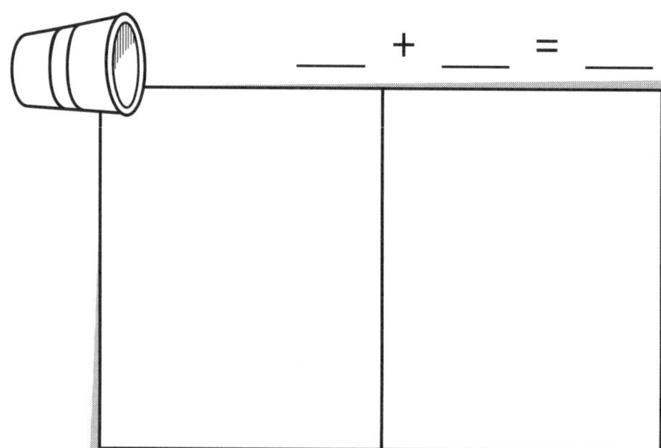

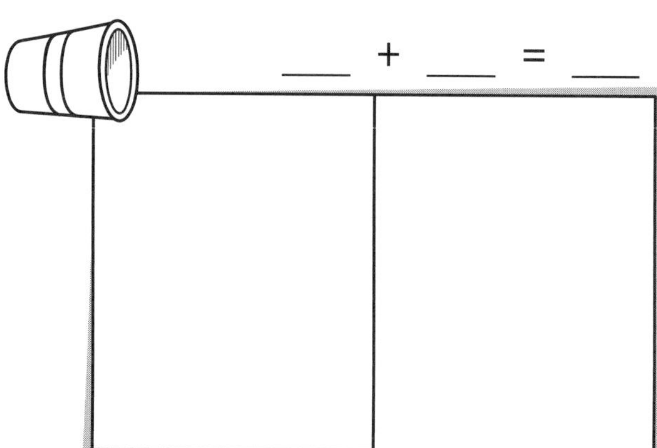

Time

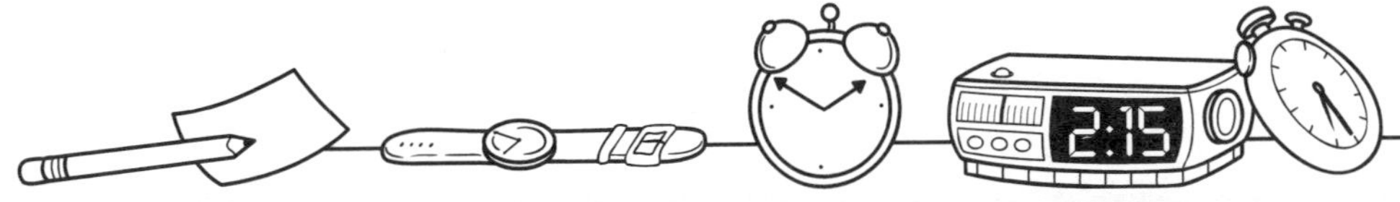

This section includes activities and literature that will help children become familiar with time, timekeeping, and even time management. Help students learn to make the most of their time with these lessons.

Time

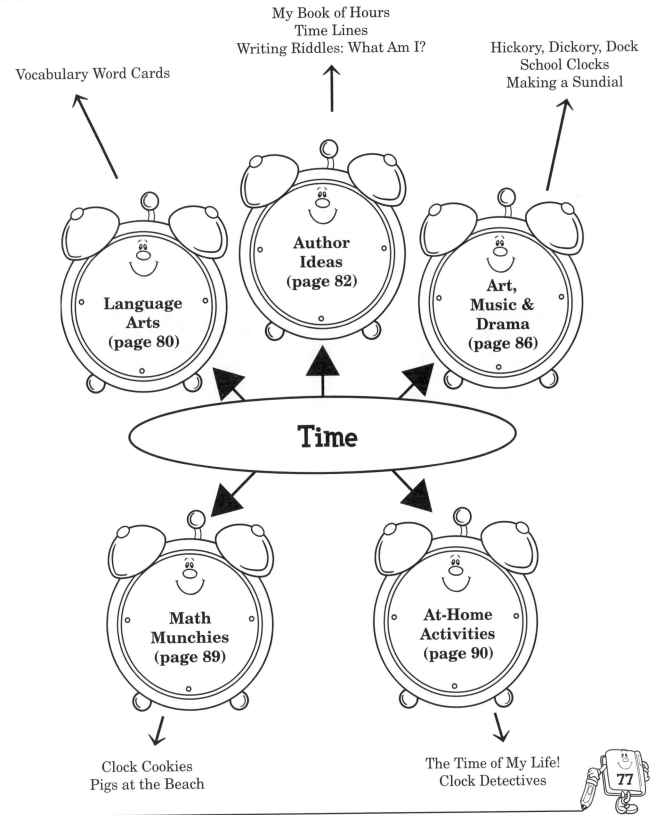

Language Arts (page 80)
- Vocabulary Word Cards

Author Ideas (page 82)
- My Book of Hours
- Time Lines
- Writing Riddles: What Am I?

Art, Music & Drama (page 86)
- Hickory, Dickory, Dock
- School Clocks
- Making a Sundial

Math Munchies (page 89)
- Clock Cookies
- Pigs at the Beach

At-Home Activities (page 90)
- The Time of My Life!
- Clock Detectives

Literature Selections

Featured Literature

The following selections are used in conjunction with the activities in this section. You may want to obtain them from your library before you start the unit. (Activities with which the books are used are listed in parentheses.)

Bear Child's Book of Hours, by Anne Rockwell (Crowell, 1987). This book shares all the things Bear Child does during the day. A clock shows the time each activity occurs, illustrating how all 24 hours of the day were spent. (My Book of Hours, page 82)

The Clock Shop, by Simon Henwood (Aurum Books for Children, 1989). This is a tale of a clock maker who has the important job of keeping everyone's clocks running on time, so everything in the town will go smoothly. (Making a Sundial, page 87; Clock Detectives, page 90)

Get Up and Go! by Stuart J. Murphy (HarperCollins, 1996). This is an introduction to time lines, as a dog keeps track of the time it takes to get ready and off to school. Suggestions for a number of activities are provided at the end of the book. (Time Lines, page 82; The Time of My Life! page 90)

Monster Goes to School, by Virginia Mueller (A. Whitman, 1991). Young Monster brags that he can tell time, but is he right? (School Clocks, page 86)

My First Look at Time, a Dorling Kindersley book (Random House, 1991). Photographs are used to illustrate everyday activities and the times they most likely occur. Pictures of objects that might be used during each activity are provided as a springboard for discussion and vocabulary development. (Clock Cookies, page 89)

Pigs on a Blanket, by Amy Axelrod (Simon & Schuster Books for Young Readers, 1996). A pig family decides to go to the beach but finds they do not get to ride the waves because of the way they have used their time. A summary is provided at the end of the book to help students see what went wrong. The author also provides a page of time facts that help clarify concepts and define terms for children. (Pigs at the Beach, page 89)

Telling Time: How to Tell Time on Digital and Analog Clocks! by Jules Older (Charlesbridge, 2000). This book introduces the concept of time and the ways we use to keep track of it from a second to a century. The author compares analog and digital clocks, explains the parts of a clock, tells how clocks help to tell time, and concludes with a poem to help remember how long things take. (Vocabulary Word Cards, page 80; Writing Riddles: What Am I? page 83)

Additional Suggested Literature

A Clock for Beany, Lisa Bassett (Dodd, Mead, 1985). Beany Bear receives a clock for his birthday, which begins a day of adventures for him.

It's About Time, Jesse Bear, and Other Rhymes, by Nancy White Carlstrom (Macmillan, 1990). A little bear explores many things throughout the day as he learns about time.

Little Rabbits' First Time Book, by Alan Baker (Kingfisher, 1999). Children will get lots of practice telling time while moving the hands of the clock included in the book as they follow the rabbits throughout their busy day. Each page includes an illustration of a digital and an analog clock to help the reader set the movable clock to the correct time.

Telling Time with Big Mama Cat, by Dan Harper (Harcourt Brace, 1998). This book follows Big Mama Cat through her day. It includes a clock with movable hands that children may use for practice in telling time.

Time for Tom, by Phil Vischer (Tommy Nelson, 1998). This VeggieTales rhyming book takes Tom Grape through his day by noting the time that he takes part in everyday activities.

Twelve Hats for Lena: A Book of Months, Karen Katz (Margaret K. McElderry Books, 2002). Lena makes a hat for each month. Students can identify holidays associated with each month.

Language Arts

Vocabulary Word Cards

Literature: *Telling Time: How to Tell Time on Digital and Analog Clocks!* by Jules Older

Materials: Index cards or reproducible from page 81 (with tagboard and scissors), resealable plastic bags or binding rings and hole punch

Activity: Read *Telling Time,* by Jules Older, to your class. It is a great resource for time vocabulary words and beginning concepts. Students will quickly learn these vocabulary words if you build in a little time each day to discuss and review them. Creating vocabulary cards for each student will help you accomplish this goal. Give each student an index card for each word that he will need to know, or use the reproducible on page 81 to copy the words onto tagboard and have students cut them apart. Keep the cards in resealable plastic bags or on rings so they will be together and ready to use.

Time Vocabulary Words

A.M.	half hour	minute hand	second
analog clock	hour	month	second hand
century	hour hand	noon	stopwatch
day	midnight	o'clock	timer
decade	millennium	P.M.	week
digital clock	minute	quarter hour	year

Here are some of the ways that you can use these cards:

- Give the definition for a word and have children "show you" the correct answer by holding up the card. You can quickly see who needs review.
- Choose three cards at random and have the children put them in alphabetical order. Have them choose another card and place it in the correct spot. Continue until all the cards are drawn.
- Write sentences with missing time words on the board. Read each sentence aloud and have the children hold up the word that is missing, or have a set of words available with magnet tape on the back for children to insert in the correct spots.
- Students can make their own bingo "cards" by randomly arranging the words in rows and columns on their desks. They should turn each card over when you say the word or its definition until a winner has completed a row across or down.
- Choose cards that are similar, such as *second*, *minute*, and *hour*. Have students arrange the words from shortest to longest time duration.
- Divide the class into teams and play tic-tac-toe. Each team may place a mark on the grid if they can correctly use a word in a sentence, answer a riddle, or give the definition of the word.

A.M.	hour hand	P.M.
analog clock	midnight	quarter hour
century	millennium	second
day	minute	second hand
decade	minute hand	stopwatch
digital clock	month	timer
half hour	noon	week
hour	o'clock	year

Author Ideas

My Book of Hours

Literature: *Bear Child's Book of Hours*, by Anne Rockwell

Materials: Construction paper, photocopier paper, clock face patterns (page 84 or 85), stapler, pencils, markers or crayons, scissors, glue

Activity: Your students may enjoy recording their daily activities in their very own Book of Hours. Conserve instructional time by making the books ahead or having a parent volunteer put the books together for you, one for each student. For each book, fold three sheets of copier paper and a sheet of construction paper in half. Place the blank sheets in the center of the construction paper cover. Staple along the fold line to complete the diary. Make copies of the clock faces, either the hour clocks or blank clock faces, for the students to use in their booklets.

After reading and discussing *Bear Child's Book of Hours*, by Anne Rockwell, distribute the hour booklets to your students. Ask them to write "My Book of Hours" on the front cover along with their names. Have students record their activities during a typical school day and either cut out and glue the corresponding hour clock on that page or fill in the blank clock face to show the correct time. You may also want to send the books home and invite parents to help students complete the pages for the hours they are at home.

Display the books on a bulletin board entitled "All about Our Day" or give the children an opportunity to share them with class members by providing a time for them to trade books to read or to show and tell about their books.

Time Lines

Literature: *Get Up and Go!* by Stuart J. Murphy

Materials: Stopwatch or clock with a second hand, paper or roll of adding machine tape, pencils

Activity: *Get Up and Go*! by Stuart J. Murphy, is a great way to introduce the concept of a time line to your students. Read the book to your class and take a few minutes to discuss the concepts presented. Children will identify with getting ready for school in the morning and will begin to see how time can be gobbled up by all of the activities that they need to accomplish in a given amount of time.

Expand upon this idea by relating it to a school activity, such as getting ready for lunch or getting ready to go home. You can easily do this by serving as a timekeeper after giving students directions for getting ready for lunch, such as the following: Clear

Time
11:00

your desks—2 minutes; Girls get lunches—1 minute; Boys get lunches—1 minute; Girls line up—1 minute; Boys line up—1 minute; Walk to the lunchroom—3 minutes. When the class returns from lunch, give each student a piece of paper to create a time line charting the time it took them to get ready for lunch. Strips of adding machine tape or shelf paper work well for this activity.

As your students begin to understand the concept of time lines by completing the previous activities, extend their knowledge by making time lines that represent longer periods of time. For example, you might make a time line for a regular school day. Next, you may want to have students chart important events during the year, dates of important historical events, or even the correct sequence for a science experiment. Display the time lines in your room or throughout the building. These activities will not only give students a way to organize and arrange dates of historical importance but will give them a better concept of time.

Writing Riddles: What Am I?

Literature: *Telling Time: How to Tell Time on Digital and Analog Clocks!* by Jules Older

Materials: Time word cards (reproducible, page 81), paper and pencils

I am a small measure of time. Sixty of me make a minute.

Activity: *Telling Time: How to Tell Time on Digital and Analog Clocks!* by Jules Older, does a great job of explaining the concept of time from the tiniest measurement to the very largest. The vocabulary and concepts presented in this book will help your students gain an understanding of time. After reading and discussing the book, give your students a tool to help them remember the time vocabulary and concepts by distributing a vocabulary word card and a half sheet of blank paper to each student. Have each student write the vocabulary word on one side of the paper and a "What Am I?" riddle on the other. To help prepare them for this task, use a remaining word card to write a riddle together. Examples might include the following:

> "I am a small measure of time. Sixty of me make a minute. What am I?" *(a second)*
>
> "I am a large measure of time. It takes 10 centuries, 100 decades, or 1,000 years to make one of me. What am I?" *(a millennium)*

Collect the riddles and keep them in a decorated coffee can or box labeled "Time Riddles." Divide the class into teams and play for points, use these riddles when you have a few extra minutes, or have children earn their places in line for lunch or dismissal by correctly answering a riddle.

Variation: Collect all of the riddles that your students have written and put them together in a classroom book. Display it on your bookshelf and allow students to borrow it when their work is done. It will be a great opportunity to review the concept of time.

Daily Diary Clocks: To the Hour

Daily Diary Clocks

Hickory, Dickory, Dock

Literature: "Hickory, Dickory, Dock" nursery rhyme or song (in a book or as a recording)

Materials: Clock manipulative for each student or team (see page 88 for a reproducible clock pattern if you do not have manipulatives)

Activity: Introduce the children's nursery rhyme, "Hickory, Dickory, Dock," to your students. After your class has become familiar with the tune, change the lyrics slightly to say, "Hickory, dickory, dock. The mouse ran up the clock. The clock struck one. The mouse ran down. What time was it?" Then ask your students to manipulate their individual clocks to read one o'clock. In this activity, students may be easily observed so you can be certain they understand where the two clock hands need to be placed to read one o'clock. Continue singing new verses, changing the time that students must show on their clocks.

Variation: This activity can be changed to a class relay game by dividing the class into teams and providing one large clock for each team. You can do this by attaching magnetic tape to clocks made from paper plates (or use the reproducible clock found on page 88) and placing the clocks on the board. Sing the verse and have a member of each team race to their clock to show the time you named. All teams with the correct answer are awarded one point and the team that finishes first receives a bonus point. Keep score with tally marks above each team's clock. To add a little drama to this activity, students going to the board could wear mouse ear headbands. Most students will not be able to "squeak by" this fun learning experience without being able to read the hours on the clock.

School Clocks

Literature: *Monster Goes to School*, by Virginia Mueller

Materials: Watercolor markers and paper

Activity: Read *Monster Goes to School*, by Virginia Mueller, to your class. When the young monster goes to school, he tells his teacher that he can tell time. He proceeds to say that there is playtime, story time, music time, lunchtime, nap time, and drawing time. He makes a very special school clock that has no hands and no numbers, and does not go "ticktock." He makes a picture clock. After discussing the book, have your students use paper and markers to create their own school picture clocks.

Variation: Make a very large circle on a piece of butcher paper using a hula hoop. Divide the circle into six parts and have the children illustrate it to create a school picture clock.

Making a Sundial

Literature: *The Clock Shop*, by Simon Henwood

Materials: Stick or dowel rod, rocks, paper and pencils

Activity: *The Clock Shop*, by Simon Henwood, gives examples of many kinds of clocks. Discuss the history of clocks with your class. Be sure to mention that, long before we had the analog and digital clocks of today, people kept track of passing time by building sundials. You may want to make a simple sundial with your students using the following directions, then discuss some of these issues: What drawbacks did these clocks have? How might they have helped us develop the clocks we have today?

Outside your classroom window might be a great place to build your sundial, since it will be easy for your class to observe throughout the day. You can construct the sundial by driving a stick or dowel rod into the ground. Be sure that you choose a sunny location, not a shady one! Place a rock at the point on the ground where the shadow falls. You may want to note the time on your classroom clock. Every hour or so, check the sundial and place a new stone at the point where the end of the stick's shadow falls. Continue to record the time and discuss observations as you go. Observe the sundial over several days or a couple weeks if possible. Record observations and discuss ideas on why this method of tracking time fell from favor.

12
1
2
3
4
5
6
7
8
9
10
11

Math Munchies

Clock Cookies

Literature: *My First Look at Time*, a Dorling Kindersley book

Materials needed: Large sugar cookies, can of frosting, chocolate chips, pretzel sticks, plastic knives, napkins

Activity: *My First Look at Time* will give your students another opportunity to practice telling time to the hour and allow them to see how telling time helps us organize and predict events of the day. After reading and discussing the book, have your students make clock cookies. This can be a simple task if you purchase large sugar cookies from a bakery. Each child will frost a cookie to serve as a clock face and then carefully arrange chocolate chips on the "clock" in place of the numbers. Start by positioning a chip for the 12, then the 6, followed by 3 and 9. Carefully place the other "in-between" numbers on the cookie. Give each child two pretzel sticks, one shorter than the other, to serve as the clock hands. Assign a time to each child and have her place the hands in the correct position. Before munching on these sweet treats, review the book and have the child who made the cookie for each time mentioned hold up her cookie to show the class.

Pigs at the Beach

Literature: *Pigs on a Blanket*, by Amy Axelrod

Materials: Beach umbrella, plastic wading pool, a variety of books with a time or beach theme, "pigs in a blanket" (miniature hot dogs wrapped in crescent rolls and baked), juice drinks, beach towels

Activity: The Pig family learns a hard lesson about using time wisely in *Pigs on a Blanket*, by Amy Axelrod. The family had hoped to spend the day at the beach but could not quite get their act together. By the time they arrived at the beach, there was not enough time left to enjoy the day. The summary at the end of the book will help your students see what went wrong. You may want to capitalize on the theme of the book and have your class earn some extra time by working harder to line up, get materials ready, clear their desks, etc., in a timely manner. "Save" this time in a "beach day account" and, when you reach your goal, celebrate!

You may do this activity indoors or outside. Make your beach day special by bringing in a beach umbrella and a plastic wading pool. Instead of filling the pool with water, fill it with books. Furnish pigs in a blanket and juice drinks. Ask parents for help! Have your students bring in their favorite beach towels so they have places to spread out as they read their favorite beach books from the pool. When you return to the classroom, have students write about their special beach day celebration in their journals.

At-Home Activities

The Time of My Life!

Literature: *Get Up and Go!* by Stuart J. Murphy

Materials: Resealable plastic bags or brown lunch bags, parent letter (reproducible, page 91), about 36 in. (90 cm) strips of adding machine tape or shelf paper

Activity: After reading and discussing *Get Up and Go!* and taking part in several time line activities, your students will be ready to create time lines of their lives with the help of their families. With a little planning and organization, this can be a fun and easy project for all.

For each child, place a copy of the parent letter from page 91 and a strip of adding machine tape in a storage bag or lunch bag. Each child will take a bag home, where, with the help of his parents, he will create a time line of his life. It will start with his birth and end with the current year. The events included "in between" are up to each child and family. The time line will need to show the date and year of each event and the child's age in months at the time. Parents may also work with their child to convert the child's age from months to years and months for each event. The time line can include photographs, drawings, pictures from magazines, writing, or any combination of these things. When the projects are completed, students are to bring their time lines back to school, where they can share them with their friends. Save room on a classroom or hallway bulletin board to display these creations.

Clock Detectives

Literature: *The Clock Shop*, by Simon Henwood

Materials: Chart paper and marker or chalkboard and chalk, activity sheet (reproducible, page 92)

Activity: After reading *The Clock Shop*, by Simon Henwood, to your class, make a list of all of the kinds of clocks mentioned in the book. Your list should include a clown clock, trumpeter clock, milkman's clock, alarm clock, church clock, and cuckoo clock. Take time to look around the classroom with your students and name the clocks that they can find, such as a wall clock, stopwatch, clock radio, VCR clock, wristwatch, etc.

Tell the children that tonight they will also be "clock detectives" at home by looking to see which clocks they may have around the house. Give each child a copy of the reproducible on page 92 to take home.

When they return their papers the next day, list all of the types of clocks the children found. Next, count the number of students who had each kind of clock and make a bar graph with this information. Which clocks were the most common? Which were the most unusual? Who found the most clocks?

Dear Parents,

We have been learning all about time, including ways that we measure it and keep track of it. One way to keep track of the passage of time is to create a time line of important events. We are counting on you to help your child complete a time line of his or her life. Inside this bag, you will find a strip of paper that can be used to create this time line. It will begin with your child's birth and end with the current year. The events that you choose to include "in between" these important dates are up to you but might include some of the following:

- Births of siblings
- A vacation or family trip
- The day your child started school. You could include the name of the school and the teacher for each grade.
- Broken bones, stitches, or operations
- When you moved into your current house
- When he or she learned to ride a bike, learned to roller blade, or mastered another skill
- A favorite holiday celebration
- When he or she began to play team sports
- Losing the first tooth
- Getting a pet
- Birthday parties or celebrations

Choose the events you and your child wish to include in the time line and place them in the correct order, being sure to write the date and year of each event. Next, help your child discover his or her age in months at the time the event took place. Beginning with your child's birth month, tally the months and count them aloud to help your child calculate his or her age. You may also work together to convert the total from months to years and months for another way to indicate your child's age at each of the important dates on the time line.

Illustrate the events with photographs, pictures from magazines, your child's drawings, or any combination of these things. Have your child return the time line to school, where he or she will be given an opportunity to share it with the class. After it has been displayed in the classroom, it will be returned to you.

As always your help and support are greatly appreciated!

Sincerely,

Child's Name:______________________________ Date:________________________

Clock Detective

Dear Parents,

Our class is learning about telling time. We have learned that there are lots of ways to tell time, as well as many different kinds of clocks. Your child has been encouraged to walk around your house tonight and list as many ways as he or she can find that your family uses to tell time. Please help your child to name these "clocks" in the space below.

Discuss this list with your child. How or why did your child select the items listed below? Together, can you find any more items used to measure time? Think creatively and include all kinds of clocks and ways to keep track of time! (Hint: Look for clocks on appliances, in drawers, in the garden, in the car, on the mantel, or on you!)

Thanks for lending a helping hand to our study of time. Your help is greatly appreciated.

Sincerely,

These are the clocks I found at my house:

____

____

____

____

____

____

____

____

____

Measurement

This section gives students valuable practice in various types of measurement, including length, weight, and comparisons.

Measurement

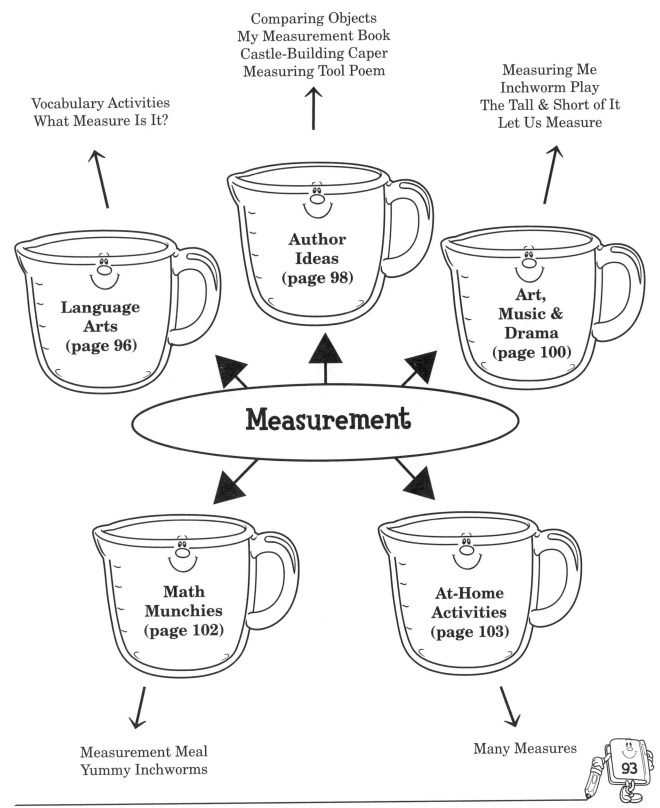

Language Arts (page 96)
- Vocabulary Activities
- What Measure Is It?

Author Ideas (page 98)
- Comparing Objects
- My Measurement Book
- Castle-Building Caper
- Measuring Tool Poem

Art, Music & Drama (page 100)
- Measuring Me
- Inchworm Play
- The Tall & Short of It
- Let Us Measure

Math Munchies (page 102)
- Measurement Meal
- Yummy Inchworms

At-Home Activities (page 103)
- Many Measures

Literature Selections

Featured Literature

The following selections are used in conjunction with the activities in this section. You may want to obtain them from your library before you start the unit. (Activities with which the books are used are listed in parentheses.)

The Best Bug Parade, by Stuart J. Murphy (HarperCollins Publishers, 1996). Bugs line up for a parade after determining their correct places. The characters make comparisons of size by big, small, long, and short. The author provides a variety of follow-up activities at the end of the book. (The Tall & Short of It, page 101)

Inchworm and a Half, by Elinor J. Pinczes (Houghton Mifflin Co., 2001). An inchworm runs into difficulty while measuring vegetables in the garden when he finds some that do not equal exactly an inch. Smaller worms come to the rescue to help measure one-half-, one-third-, and one-quarter-inch lengths. (Inchworm Play, page 100; Yummy Inchworms, page 102)

Knowabout Length, by Henry Pluckrose (F. Watts, 1988). This book introduces the concept of measurement. It talks about standard measurements and tools for measuring, and provides students opportunities to make predictions and arrange objects in order by size. Photographs help illustrate each concept discussed. (What Measure Is It? page 96; Measuring Me, page 100)

The Long and Short of It, by Cheryl Nathan and Lisa McCourt (BridgeWater Books, 1998). This book compares the sizes and shapes of animals and their parts. (Comparing Objects, page 98)

Me and the Measure of Things, by Joan Sweeney (Crown Publishers, 2001). This is an introduction to weights and measures. It gives examples of the tools needed for each kind of measurement and ways that the measurement is helpful in everyday life. An illustrated table of weights and measures can be found at the end of the book. (Vocabulary Activities, page 96; My Measurement Book, page 98)

Measuring Penny, by Loreen Leedy (Henry Holt, 1997). Lisa learns about measurement by measuring her dog, Penny, with all kinds of units of measure from inches to pounds to dog biscuits. (What Measure Is It? page 96; Measurement Meal, page 102; Many Measures, page 103)

Super Sand Castle Saturday, by Stuart J. Murphy (HarperCollins Publishers, 1999). Children who entered the sand castle-building contest at the beach discover the problem with nonstandard measures when they try to predict the winner of each category of the contest. (Castle-Building Caper, page 99)

Twelve Snails to One Lizard: A Tale of Mischief and Measurement, by Susan Hightower (Simon and Schuster Books for Young Readers, 1997). Bubba the bullfrog decides to help Milo the beaver more accurately measure the branches he needs to build his dam. Milo is frustrated by Bubba's suggestions to estimate the length of the log with snails, lizards, and snakes until Bubba remembers he has a yardstick. This is a good introduction to the inch, foot, and yard and their relationships. (Measuring Tool Poem, page 99)

Additional Suggested Literature

Bigger, Better, Best! by Stuart J. Murphy (HarperCollins Publishers, 2002). In this story, the siblings are always arguing about who has the biggest and best of everything. They use sheets of paper to measure the windows and rooms in the family's new home and discover that objects can be different shapes but have the same area. Ideas for measuring activities are provided by the author at the end of the book.

How Tall, How Short, How Far Away, by David A. Adler (Holiday House, 1999). Adler discusses the early history of measuring in Egypt and Rome and what measures were used. The book explores standard and nonstandard measures as well as the the metric system and systems that use inches and pounds.

Math Counts: Length, by Henry Pluckrose (Children's Press, 1995). This book uses photographs to introduce the concept of length. Different measures of length are discussed as well as standard and nonstandard measurements. The difference between height and length is also explored.

Measurement, by Sara Pistoia (Child's World, 2003). This book discusses various measurements and the best tool to use to take each measurement. It also discusses the necessity to have standard units of measure.

Measurement Mania: Games and Activities That Make Math Easy and Fun, by Lynette Long (Wiley, 2001). This book is full of games and activities that will capture your students' interest and clarify math concepts.

My First Look at Sizes (Dorling Kindersley, 2001). Photographs in this book will enable children to develop a better understanding of size by providing an opportunity to compare the familiar objects pictured on each page. Their vocabulary of comparison words will also increase because of the words printed throughout the book.

Size: Many Ways to Measure, by Michele Koomen (Bridgestone Books, 2001). Photographs are used to introduce the concept of size by exploring length, height, weight, and volume. Examples of nonstandard measurements help students see the problems that arise when standard units of measure are not employed. A glossary of terms is provided at the end of the book.

Take Off with Measuring, by Sally Hewitt (Raintree Steck-Vaughn, 1996). This book explores different ways objects are measured using length, weight, and volume. Photographs illustrate the concepts. Children are given opportunities to participate in book activities by estimating, predicting, and measuring objects.

Why We Measure, by Janine Scott (Compass Point Books, 2003). This book uses photographs to illustrate the importance of measuring in everyday life. The author explores many different reasons to measure accurately as well as different ways measurements are taken.

Vocabulary Activities

Literature: *Me and the Measure of Things*, by Joan Sweeney

Materials: Reproducible from page 97 (with tagboard and scissors), resealable plastic bags or binding rings and hole punch

Activity: *Me and the Measure of Things*, by Joan Sweeney, is an excellent book to share with the class to introduce the concepts of weight and measurement. The book begins by discussing the need to understand weights and measures and how they can be used in everyday life. It gives examples of measuring dry products, liquids, the weight and length of objects, and farmers' produce and concludes with an illustrated weights and measures table that will serve as a great reference for your class.

Practice makes perfect when it comes to mastering vocabulary. Make time to practice and review measurement words. Provide your students with their own word cards by giving them copies of the measurement words reproducible on page 97 (copy onto tagboard or heavy paper for durability). Have students cut the cards apart and keep them safe and handy in plastic storage bags or punch holes in the cards to place on rings, so they will be ready to pull out and use at a moment's notice.

After the students have made their cards, hold up an object or picture, or say the name of an object that will be measured. Have students hold up the word card that would be the best unit of measure or measurement tool to use for the job. For example, you might say:

- "What measurement word would I use to describe the distance between New York City and Washington, D. C.? (*mile, kilometer*)
- "What tool would I use to measure the top of my desk?" (*yardstick*, *meterstick*, *tape measure*)

What Measure Is It?

Literature: *Measuring Penny*, by Loreen Leedy; or *Knowabout Length*, by Henry Pluckrose

Materials: Chalkboard and chalk or chart paper and marker, index cards in at least two colors

Activity: After you have read a book about measurement, such as *Measuring Penny*, by Loreen Leedy, or *Knowabout Length*, by Henry Pluckrose, take a few minutes to review the units of measure discussed in the book. Write each unit of measurement on a white index card. On different colored cards, write or paste pictures of some of the things that could be measured with that unit. Place the cards in a small bag or box. When it is time to play, put the index cards labled with the units of measure at the top of the chart paper. Have children or teams select a colored card and place it in the column of the correct measurement term. Individuals and teams will benefit from the friendly competition of this practice activity.

bushel	meter	quart
centimeter	meterstick	scale
cup	mile	tablespoon
foot	milliliter	tape measure
gallon	millimeter	teaspoon
inch	ounce	ton
kilometer	peck	weigh
liter	pint	yard
measure	pound	yardstick

Author Ideas

Comparing Objects

Literature: *The Long and Short of It*, by Cheryl Nathan and Lisa McCourt

Activity: Read *The Long and Short of It*, by Cheryl Nathan and Lisa McCourt, to the class. The book compares animals using the words "long" and "short" to describe the sizes of the animals and their body parts. Discuss how using these words helped the authors better describe the animals. Make a list of other word pairs that could be used to compare things and give a better description and understanding of them. Your list might include the following: small and large, bright and dark, heavy and light, tall and short, and wide and narrow.

Use these words to practice comparing each other, animals, or other things in the classroom.

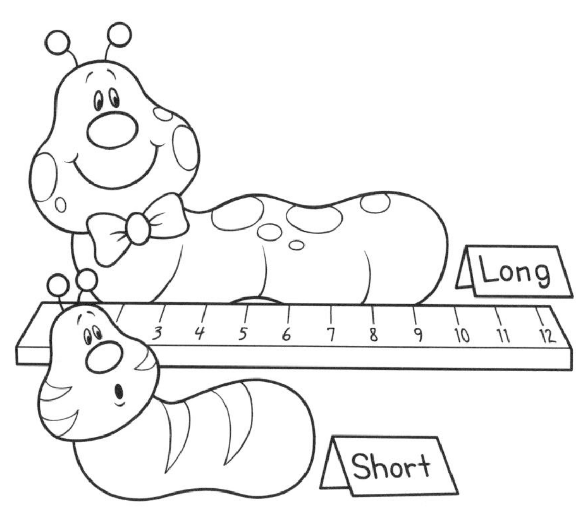

My Measurement Book

Literature: *Me and the Measure of Things*, by Joan Sweeney

Materials: Materials needed to make student books (paper, construction paper, stapler, pencils, crayons or markers)

Activity: Read *Me and the Measure of Things*, by Joan Sweeney, with your students, discussing the concepts and vocabulary from the book. Spend some time looking at the measurement table at the end of the book. Then, use this book as a model for your students to create their own books.

To create a measurement book, fold several pieces of paper in half and staple them together with a construction paper cover. On each page, students may illustrate an object and, on the facing page, describe with words and pictures how they would measure the item and the tool they would use.

Castle-Building Caper

Literature: *Super Sand Castle Saturday*, by Stuart J. Murphy

Materials: Math journals or paper, pencils

Activity: *Super Sand Castle Saturday*, by Stuart J. Murphy, is a book about a day at beach and a sand castle-building contest. The children who participated in the contest used nonstandard measures as they worked on their castles and thought that they had figured out who the winner for each category would be. Imagine their surprise when the castles were measured with a standard measure! After reading and discussing the book, have the students use the story as a springboard to write in their math journals. Some story starters might include the following:

- One day last summer, my family went to the beach and we saw the biggest . . .
- If you are going to measure with spoons, be sure that . . .
- When you build a sand castle, you need to remember to . . .

Measuring Tool Poem

Literature: *Twelve Snails to One Lizard: A Tale of Michief and Measurement*, by Susan Hightower

Materials: Paper and pencils

Activity: *Twelve Snails to One Lizard: A Tale of Michief and Measurement*, by Susan Hightower, helps students see the importance of using the right tools to measure accurately. Milo the beaver would have been saved much frustration when measuring logs for his dam if Bubba the bullfrog would have lent him his yardstick in the beginning instead of telling him to use squirmy animals to measure. Read the following poem aloud:

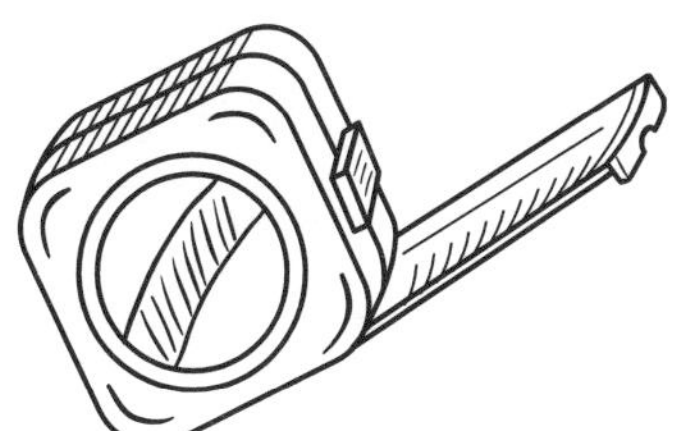

Measuring Tools

Whenever you need to measure,
The right tool is surely a treasure.
A ruler can measure an inch,
Even twelve of them; it's a cinch!
If you want to measure feet,
A yardstick has three to make it complete.
A tape measure measures around.
It is a handy tool, I have found!

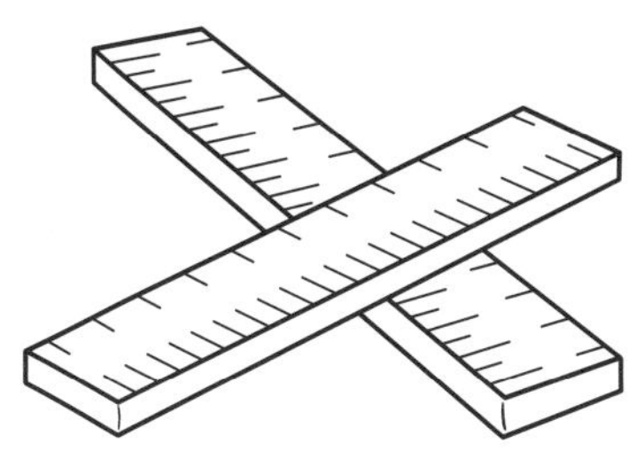

Variation: Encourage students to change the rhyming words in this poem to describe other measuring tools and their uses or they may write their own measurement poems.

Art, Music & Drama

Measuring Me

Literature: *Knowabout Length*, by Henry Pluckrose

Materials: Rulers, crayons or markers, tape measures, scissors, pencils, a large piece of butcher paper for each child

Activity: The book *Knowabout Length*, by Henry Pluckrose, will help your class to see why measuring is important and all the ways that we use measurements in our lives. They will explore standard and nonstandard units of measure and will discover tools that make measuring easier. After reading and discussing the book, let students work with partners to measure themselves.

The student pairs will take turns lying on pieces of butcher paper while their partners trace their bodies' outlines. After the children have been traced, invite them to add facial features, hair, and clothes to their outlines. When this step is completed, the students will begin to measure each other with the tape measures you provide. Be sure to give them a list of the parts they are to measure and clear directions on how to record the results on their outline figures. Display the figures in your classroom or in the hallway. You may want to line them up from shortest to tallest or tallest to shortest. When you are ready to take down the display, roll them up and send them home for bedroom decorations or keepsakes to remind the parents and children of their size "way back when."

Inchworm Play

Literature: *Inchworm and a Half*, by Elinor J. Pinczes

Materials: Construction paper, pencils, markers, glue, scissors, tape, rulers, video camera and videotape (optional)

Activity: Students are sure to enjoy the book *Inchworm and a Half*, by Elinor J. Pinczes, and will learn a great deal about measuring thanks to the inchworm and his little friends. Let students share what they have learned by making the book into a play. Invite students to create their own "inchworms" by cutting out circles from construction paper. (You may wish to provide circle templates for them to trace around.) Students can create a variety of lengths depending upon the number of circles they glue together for each inchworm. After using markers to add details such as eyes and spots, students may tape their characters onto rulers. Provide props such as plastic vegetables or fruits for the inchworms to measure and your students are ready for their first performance. Students from a neighboring classroom might enjoy watching your students perform. Parents would also be willing guests. If possible, videotape the show so that parents who are unable to attend the live performance can borrow the tape to watch the inchworm and his friends measure the vegetables in the garden.

The Tall & Short of It

Literature: *The Best Bug Parade*, by Stuart J. Murphy

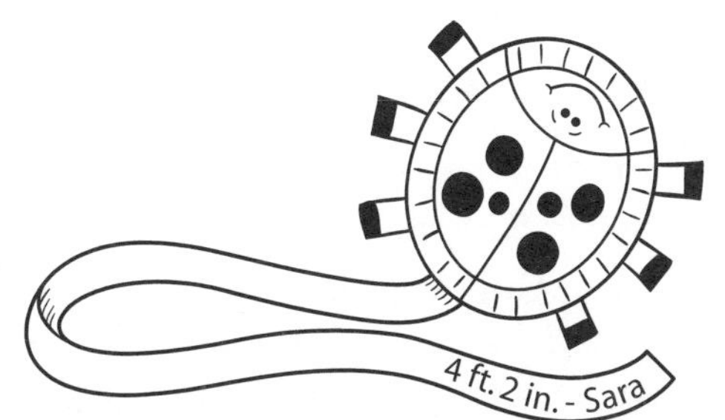

Materials: Scale with a height attachment, growth chart, or masking tape and tape measure; scissors; adding machine tape; pencils; chart paper or chalkboard; paper plates (optional)

Activity: After reading and discussing *The Best Bug Parade*, by Stuart J. Murphy, have your students begin preparing for their own parade. Determine the height of each child in your class by using a doctor's scale with a height attachment or by using a growth chart. (If you do not have either of these, use a piece of masking tape attached to a door or wall with feet and inches marked, or temporarily affix a tape measure vertically to a wall or door frame.) Once each child has her measurement number, she can work with a partner to cut a piece of adding machine tape to this length. Each child should write her height either in inches, feet and inches, or centimeters and add her name to the tape. When all of the students have created their tapes, place the strips in order from shortest to tallest. Make a bar graph with the results. What can be learned from the graph? What height was the tallest? What height was the shortest? Which height was the most common?

If time allows, have students create paper plate bugs to which they can attach their strips. While holding the paper plates, they can march around the classroom in their own best bug parade.

Let Us Measure

Materials: Measurement tools, pictures of objects, chart paper and marker

Activity: We all use measurements of some kind on a daily basis. Ask your students how their parents use measurements every day as they care for their families or do their jobs. Record the students' ideas on the chart paper. Have an assortment of measurement tools available for the students to examine. To help them understand what it means to convert measurements, demonstrate this process. For example, show how 12 inches is the same length as 1 foot or that 10 millimeters equals 1 centimeter.

Memorizing measurement tables is fun when facts are set to music. Use the song below to help students remember important measurement information and then invite them to write their own verses.

Let Us Measure
Tune: "London Bridge"

Twelve inches make a foot,
Make a foot, make a foot.
Twelve inches make a foot,
Let us measure!

Three feet make a yard,
Make a yard, make a yard,
Three feet make a yard,
Let us measure!

Other ideas for verses include:
Ten millimeters make a centimeter, . . .; Two cups make a pint, . . .; and so on.

Math Munchies

Measurement Meal

Literature: *Measuring Penny*, by Loreen Leedy

Materials: Foot-long hot dogs with buns and condiments, cupcakes, coconut, food coloring, string licorice, jelly beans, paper plates, utensils, napkins

Activity: Culminate your study of measurement by rereading the book *Measuring Penny*, by Loreen Leedy, and reviewing the concept of standard and nonstandard units of measure. After your discussion, have students partake in a Measurement Meal consisting of foot-long hot dogs and an inchworm made from cupcakes decorated with colored coconut, string licorice legs, and jelly bean eyes. What a yummy way to "measure" students' mastery of this concept!

Yummy Inchworms

Literature: *Inchworm and a Half*, by Elinor J. Pinczes

Materials: 1" strips of paper, ruler, finger-shaped (oblong) cream-filled snack cakes, jelly beans or chocolate chips, canned frosting

Activity: Read and discuss *Inchworm and a Half*, by Elinor J. Pinczes. The children will enjoy the story of the inchworm and his smaller friends who helped him measure the vegetables in his garden. Give each child two strips of paper that are each 1" in length so that she can conceptualize the size of the inchworm. Have children fold one of their papers in half to see the size of the half-inch worm and then fold it in half again to see the size of the quarter-inch worm. Fold the second piece of paper into three equal sections to make it the correct size for the one-third-inch worm. Have your class look at rulers to see how they are marked in these increments.

At the end of your discussion, give each child a snack cake and invite her to add eyes to her "inchworm" by putting a small amount of frosting on two jellybeans or chocolate chips and attaching them to the cake. It might be fun to take photographs of the work in progress as well a group picture of students with their very delicious friends.

Many Measures

Literature: *Measuring Penny*, by Loreen Leedy

Materials: Chalkboard and chalk or chart paper and marker, activity sheet (reproducible, page 104), large resealable plastic bag, paper clips, ruler, craft sticks, 36 in. (to represent yardstick) or 1 m (to represent meterstick) lengths of string, dog biscuit

Activity: To prepare students for this take-home project read *Measuring Penny*, by Loreen Leedy to the class. The students will easily relate to Penny, the little dog that was measured by her owner in many different ways. Discuss standard and nonstandard units of measure and list examples of each on the chalkboard. What are some of the things that were used in the story to measure Penny and her friends? Your list might include the following:

Standard Units of Measure

inch	ounce	kilogram
centimeter	gram	pound
teaspoon	mile	kilometer
milliliter	liter	gallon

Nonstandard Units of Measure

dog biscuit

cotton swab

me (to my waist, knee, shoulder, elbow, head)

Let students practice measuring with standard and nonstandard units in class. Give each student or pair of students a list of classroom objects that they are to measure and a large resealable plastic bag containing a paper clip, ruler, craft stick, length of string (same length as yardstick or meterstick), and dog biscuit.

Students will work individually, with a partner, or with a small group to measure each object listed on their papers with one standard and one nonstandard unit of measure and record the results on their papers. Set a timer and let the measuring begin! When the buzzer goes off, compare results and record them on a chart, on the board, or on an overhead projector.

As a follow-up activity, have each student take home the bag containing the measuring units along with a list of objects (see page 104) they are to measure in the same manner. Reward students for participating in this project with a small treat and be sure to hang their papers on a bulletin board for all to see.

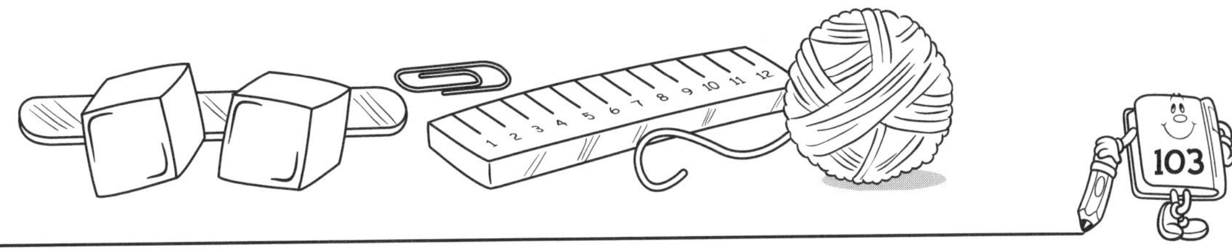

Name: ______________________ Date: ______________

Many Measures

Measure the objects. Put an **X** above the columns of standard units of measure.

		paper clip	ruler	craft stick	string	dog biscuit
1. your bed	height					
	width					
2. television	height					
	width					
3. kitchen table	height					
	width					
4. sofa	height					
	width					
5. refrigerator	height					
	width					

Money

Strong money skills are essential in everyday life, so use these activities and stories to start building those skills in your students now.

Money

Language Arts (page 108)
- Lunch Money
- Going to the Store
- Coins, Coins, Coins
- Clipping Coupons

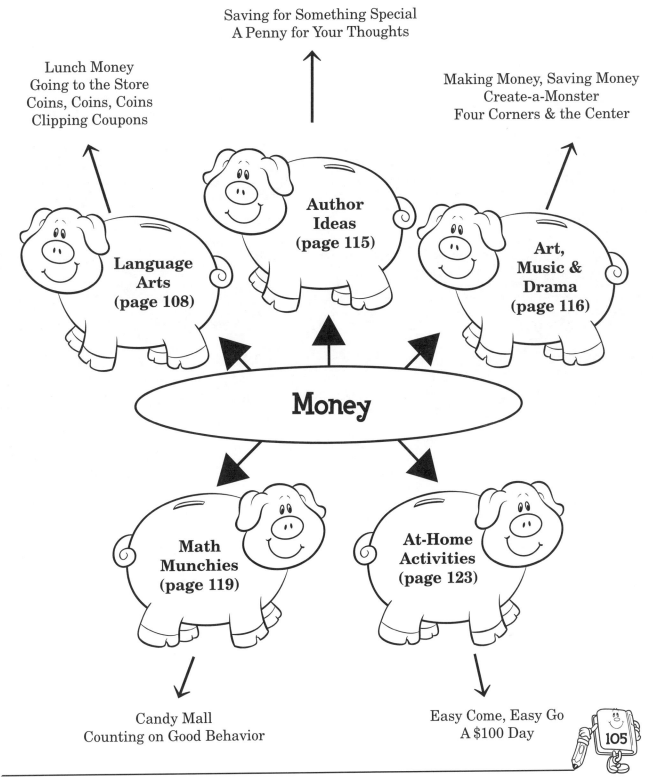

Author Ideas (page 115)
- Saving for Something Special
- A Penny for Your Thoughts

Art, Music & Drama (page 116)
- Making Money, Saving Money
- Create-a-Monster
- Four Corners & the Center

Math Munchies (page 119)
- Candy Mall
- Counting on Good Behavior

At-Home Activities (page 123)
- Easy Come, Easy Go
- A $100 Day

Literature Selections

Featured Literature

The following selections are used in conjunction with the activities in this section. You may want to obtain them from your library before you start the unit. (Activities with which the books are used are listed in parentheses.)

26 Letters and 99 Cents, by Tana Hoban (Greenwillow Books, 1987). Learn the alphabet and then turn the book over to reread it and count from 1 to 99 with different combinations of coins. (Coins, Coins, Coins, page 109)

Alexander Who Used to Be Rich Last Sunday, by Judith Viorst (Atheneum, 1978). Alexander gets a dollar from his grandparents and thinks he is rich. Each of his adventures costs him a bit of the dollar and soon he no longer has any money. (Easy Come, Easy Go, page 123)

The Berenstain Bears' Trouble with Money, by Stan and Jan Berenstain (Random House, 1983). The Berenstain Bears explore the concept of earning and saving money in this story. Students will also learn various figures of speech such as "money that grows on trees" and being "made of money." (Making Money, Saving Money, page 116)

The Frogs Wore Red Suspenders: Rhymes, by Jack Prelutsky (Greenwillow Books, 2002). Here is another fantastic poetry book by Prelutsky! Students will enjoy these poems—some silly, some nonsense, but all fun! (Going to the Store, page 108)

The Hundred Penny Box, by Sharon Bell Mathis (Puffin Books, 1986). Michael's great-great-aunt is 100 years old. She has a box containing one penny representing each year, and she has a story for each penny. Michael intercedes when his mother wants to discard the box. This book is a Newbery Honor Book. (A Penny for Your Thoughts, page 115)

Lunch Money and Other Poems about School, by Carol Diggory Shields (Dutton Children's Books, 1995). This is a good poetry book for any primary classroom. The author uses rhyme, humor, and common school concepts in these fun poems about recess, lunch, teachers, and students. (Lunch Money, page 108)

The Monster Money Book, by Loreen Leedy (Holiday House, 1992). The Monster Club has determined that they have money in their account. As they try to decide how to spend the money, concepts such as saving, profits, and budgets are introduced. (Create-a-Monster, page 117)

Pigs Go to Market: Fun with Math and Shopping, by Amy Axelrod (Simon & Schuster Books for Young Readers, 1997). Mrs. Pig wins a five-minute shopping spree at the supermarket and the Pig family goes shopping for a big Halloween bash. (Clipping Coupons, page 109; Candy Mall, page 119)

The Purse, by Kathy Caple (Houghton Mifflin, 1986). Katie spends all of her money to buy a new purse and then has no money to keep in it. (Saving for Something Special, page 115)

Reese's Pieces: Count by Fives, by Jerry Pallotta (Scholastic, 2000). Toy trucks pick up the first ten pieces of Reese's Pieces® candies, one piece at a time, but decide to speed things up when it begins to rain. They count the remaining pieces by fives to 100. (Counting on Good Behavior, page 120)

Additional Suggested Literature

Arthur's Funny Money, by Lillian Hoban (Harper & Row, 1981). Arthur tries to earn money by completing various tasks.

Benny's Pennies, by Pat Brisson (Doubleday Books for Young Readers, 1993). Benny McBride has five shiny pennies and is determined to spend all of them. Throughout the day, he finds five wonderful gifts to share with his family. The simple text is accompanied by torn and cut paper collage illustrations.

The Coin Counting Book, by Rozanne Lanczak Williams (Charlesbridge, 2001). Easy text and photograph-style illustrations make this a great book to use with young students to introduce coins and bills and their values.

If You Made a Million, by David M. Schwartz (Lothrop, Lee & Shepard Books, 1989). This book demonstrates the different combinations of coins and bills that are equal. Children will also be introduced to other concepts related to money such as bank accounts, interest, and spending.

Jelly Beans for Sale, by Bruce McMillan (Scholastic, 1996). McMillan uses photographs of money and jelly beans to illustrate the various coin equivalencies a buyer could use to purchase jelly beans.

Sluggers' Car Wash, by Stuart J. Murphy (HarperCollins, 2002). The characters in this story try to raise money to buy new uniforms for the big baseball game.

Language Arts

Lunch Money

Literature: "Lunch Money," from *Lunch Money and Other Poems about School*, by Carol Diggory Shields

Materials: Reproducibles from pages 110 and 111 or 112, scissors, crayons, chart paper and marker

Activity: Young students are active students! Sometimes you need an activity that encourages movement and whole-class participation. Poetry and math? You bet! Carol Diggory Shields has written a poem called "Lunch Money" as part of her poetry book, *Lunch Money and Other Poems about School*. This is a great poem to use with students who are learning to recognize coins and bills.

First, provide each student with a copy of the U. S. or Canadian coin. Give students time to cut out and color each coin or bill. As they are cutting out their pieces, write the poem on chart paper or the chalkboard. Read the poem aloud to the students as you point to each word. Then, give them an opportunity to read it together with you. When you feel students are familiar with the poem, have them continue the choral reading exercise, but tell them that this time they should hold up the corresponding picture as they recite each part of the poem. For example, when the students say the word "nickel" in the poem, they should hold up their nickel cutouts. As the children read the poem, you will clearly be able to see which students can accurately identify the coins and bills. Invite students to try writing their own stanza featuring other coins and objects and add it to the poem.

Going to the Store

Literature: "I Went to the Store," from *The Frogs Wore Red Suspenders: Rhymes*, by Jack Prelutsky

Materials: Chart paper and marker, reproducibles from pages 113 and 114, pencils

Activity: Another great poem to use in your money unit is Jack Prelutsky's "I Went to the Store." This whimsical rhyming poem describes a trip to the store gone bad. Read the poem to the class. Make sure the students understand the meanings of any new vocabulary words, and take some time to discuss the rhyming pattern.

Copy the poem onto chart paper so the students can read along with you. Use the reproducible on page 113 to model adding money. As you read the poem, identify the cost of each item on the reproducible and add the amounts. Explain to the students that they should only add the items that were actually sold. Challenge your students to calculate the total bill of the shopping trip.

Finally, give your young poets an opportunity to create their own versions of this fun rhyme. Provide each student with a copy of the poem, "I Went to the Mall," on page 114. Explain to the students that the rhyming pattern is similar to Prelutsky's poem, and the students will need to complete each stanza by filling in the appropriate words of the pictures on that page. When the students have completed the poem, they will be able to calculate the total cost of the shopping trip by adding the prices. Alternatively, encourage students to write their own versions of the poem "I Went to the Store."

Coins, Coins, Coins

Literature: *26 Letters and 99 Cents*, by Tana Hoban

Materials: Coin manipulatives, paper, pencils

Activity: As students begin to differentiate between the monetary amounts of coins, they can also identify the unique characteristics of each coin. Share the book *26 Letters and 99 Cents*, by Tana Hoban, with your students and then divide your class into six groups. Prepare six sets of coins, each containing one penny, one dime, one nickel, one quarter, one half-dollar, and one silver dollar. Give each group a set of coins. Allow time for the students to examine the coins and talk about how each one is different from the others.

Then, assign each group a specific denomination of coin that the group will examine and compare to the other coins. Provide each group with a sheet of paper that is folded lengthwise to create two columns. Instruct the groups to write the word "same" at the top of one column and "different" at the top of the other column. Ask each group to list the characteristics that make its coin different from all the other coins in the "different" column. For example, the group that is examining the penny may identify color as a distinguishing factor. Groups should also list the similar characteristics in the "same" column. Remind students to identify only the characteristics that their coin shares with all of the other coins. When every group has had time to complete its list, give each group an opportunity to report the findings to the rest of the class.

Clipping Coupons

Literature: *Pigs Go to Market: Fun with Math and Shopping*, by Amy Axelrod

Materials: Newspaper grocery coupons, scissors, reproducible from page 113, paper, pencils

Activity: Many students have seen their parents use coupons. This activity will give them an opportunity to understand how coupons help the buyer save money. Read *Pigs Go to Market*, by Amy Axelrod to the class. Clip enough coupons from the newspaper so that you can give each child at least two coupons. Then distribute a copy of the reproducible on page 113 to each student. Ask students to determine how much money each coupon would be worth if they purchased the product featured on the coupon. Then ask them to find at least one item on the reproducible that could be purchased with the savings. Write the following sentence skeletons on the board:

My coupon is worth ____________. I can buy __________ with the money I save.

Give students time to complete the sentences on notebook paper. Students can then exchange coupons and repeat the process.

IN GOD WE TRUST
LIBERTY
2003
UNITED STATES OF AMERICA
E • PLURIBUS • UNUM •
ONE CENT
LIBERTY
IN GOD WE TRUST
2004
UNITED STATES OF AMERICA
E PLURIBUS UNUM
ONE DIME 
FEDERAL RESERVE NOTE
THE UNITED STATES OF AMERICA
FIVE
CL78434550 47B
FIVE DOLLARS
G
5

LIBERTY
IN GOD WE
TRUST
2004

IN GOD WE TRUST
LIBERTY
2002

UNITED STATES OF AMERICA
E PLURIBUS
UNUM
QUARTER DOLLAR

E PLURIBUS UNUM
MONTICELLO
FIVE CENTS
UNITED STATES OF AMERICA

5
CANADA
CINQ • FIVE
DOLLARS
5
BANK OF CANADA • BANQUE DU CANADA

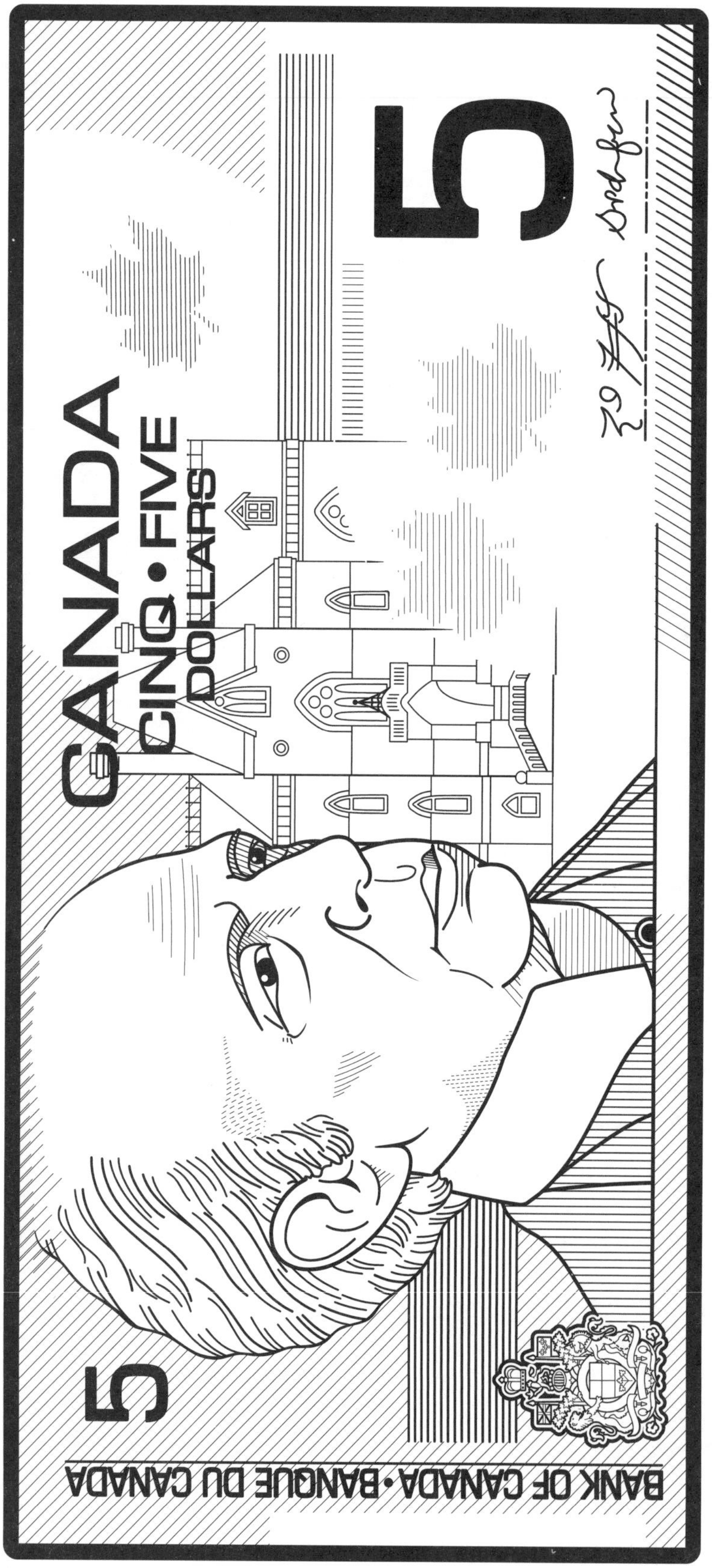

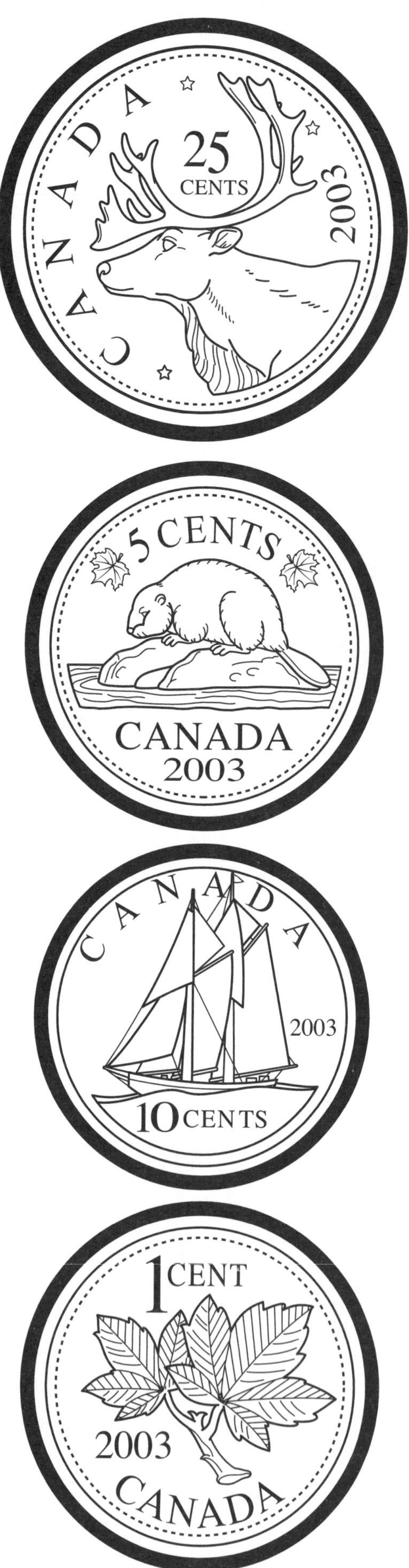

CANADA
25
CENTS
2003

5 CENTS
CANADA
2003

CANADA
2003
10 CENTS

1 CENT
2003
CANADA

$8.00
$5.00
5¢
95¢
25¢
BREAD
$1.65
$1.50
MILK
$1.85
GLUE
65¢
$6.25
90¢
BUTTER
35¢
75¢
BEANS
90¢
$1.00
10¢

Name: ______________________ Date: ______________________

Going to the Store

Directions: Fill in the blanks with words that rhyme. Use the pictures to help you. Add to find out the actual total cost of the shopping trip.

I Went to the Mall

I went to the mall
To buy a ball and a bat,
But the shelves were all bare
So they sold me a __________.
I tried to buy shoes
And a cool pair of jeans,
But they said they were out
And they sold me some ____________.
I wanted a football
Striped silver and blue.
They said they had none
So they sold me some ____________.
They didn't have paper
Not one pencil or __________.
I'll never go back to
That mall again!

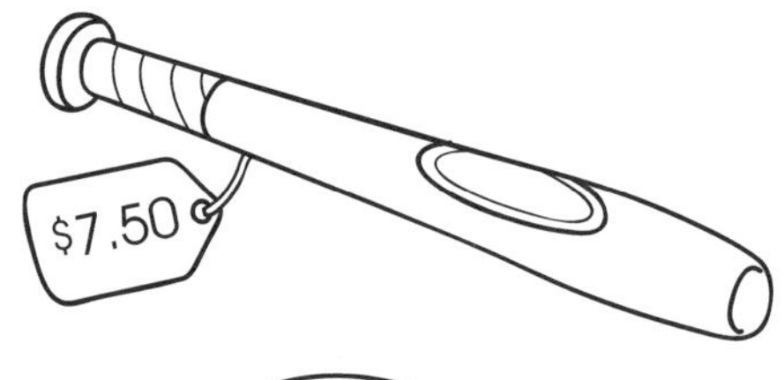

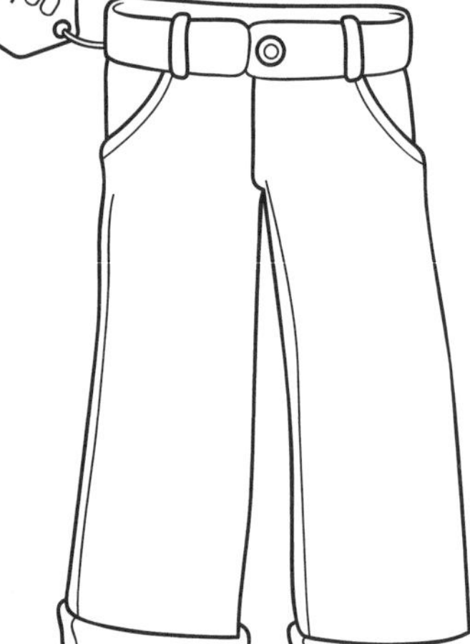

Author Ideas

Saving for Something Special

Literature: *The Purse*, by Kathy Caple

Materials: Pencils, journals or paper

Activity: Even young children can develop an appreciation for saving up for something special. Share the story of *The Purse*, by Kathy Caple, about a young girl named Katie who keeps her money in a tin bandage box. When she spends her savings on a new purse, she realizes that she no longer has money to put in the new purse. As you read this story to your students, keep track of the money the character earns. Periodically throughout the story, stop and ask students to add up her earnings. When you finish the story, discuss it with your students. Ask them to share a time when they were saving their money for something special. Then give them time to write in their journals. Here are some story starters you could provide:

- I'm saving every penny I earn so I can buy . . .
- If I could buy anything in the whole world, I would buy . . .

Be sure to give the students an opportunity to share their writing with the class.

A Penny for Your Thoughts

Literature: *The Hundred Penny Box*, by Sharon Bell Mathis

Materials: A supply of pennies, pencils, journals or paper

Activity: Storytelling and journal writing go hand in hand with this activity based on the book, *The Hundred Penny Box*. Read and discuss the story with the students. Then give each student a penny to examine closely. Talk about the year that is printed on the penny and explain that every penny made indicates the year it was minted. Allow the students to work in groups of three or four. Give each group a small container of pennies. Ask them to try to find one penny that was minted in each year that they have been alive. For example, if a student was born in 1997, he should look for pennies minted in 1997, 1998, 1999, and so on to the current year. Instruct the students to arrange the pennies they have found in chronological order. Then, tell them to record those years in their journals and write one special event for each year (e.g., "In the year 1997, I was born. In the year 1998, I learned to walk."). It may be appropriate for younger students to simply record the years in their journals and draw a picture of a special event that occurred in each year. Older students may be able to write a few sentences or a paragraph for each year. Encourage students to share this journal entry with their parents and ask for additional information about these important years.

Making Money, Saving Money

Literature: *The Berenstain Bears' Trouble with Money*, by Stan and Jan Berenstain

Materials: Chart paper and marker, reproducible from page 118, small containers to serve as banks (e.g., tissue boxes, potato chip cans, etc.), materials for decorating (e.g., construction paper, wrapping paper, photographs, pictures from magazines, etc.), markers or crayons, glue, scissors

Activity: The concept of money is often a difficult one for some students. Learning to have an appreciation for money and what it means to earn and save money are ideas that you can discuss with your students. Share Stan and Jan Berenstain's book *The Berenstain Bears' Trouble with Money* with the class. Then engage the children in a class discussion about different ways that they can earn money. Some students may comment that they receive a weekly or monthly allowance. (Caution students to not share specific details about their allowances.) Point out that most family members are responsible for household chores, and some children earn their allowances by completing various tasks. From this class discussion, create a chart that lists a variety of things children can do to earn money.

Give your students the opportunity to create special "banks" that they can take home for storing their savings. Use the reproducible letter on page 118 to explain the project to parents, inviting them to send small containers and materials with which to create and decorate the banks. Students can use small, square tissue boxes, potato chip cans, or any inexpensive containers for saving their money. (Remind students that if a container without a removable lid or an opening for retrieving the money is used, it may have to be broken apart to remove the money.) Let the students decorate their containers with the collected materials.

Create-a-Monster

Literature: *The Monster Money Book*, by Loreen Leedy

Materials: Modeling clay, decorative materials to serve as monster features, index cards and marker

Activity: Nurture your students' creativity with this fun activity after reading Leedy's *The Monster Money Book* to the class. The book features a Monster Club that has money in the treasury account to spend. As the characters decide how they will spend the money, the author introduces concepts such as budgets, saving, profits, etc.

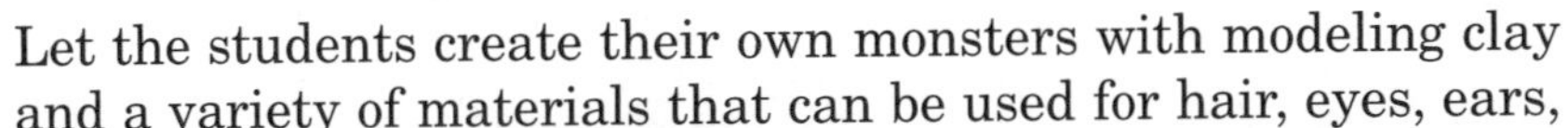

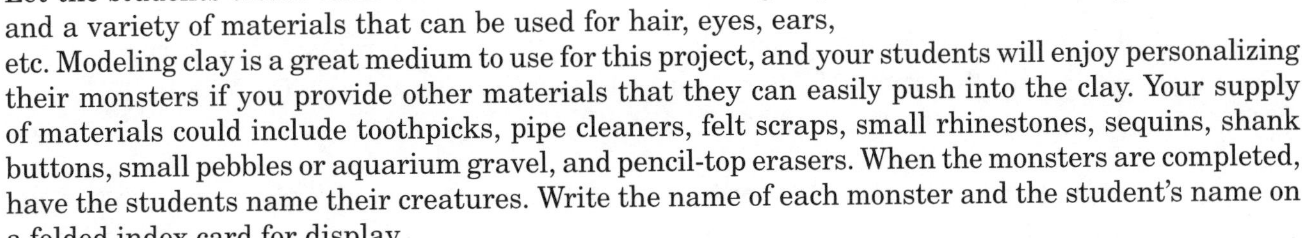

Let the students create their own monsters with modeling clay and a variety of materials that can be used for hair, eyes, ears, etc. Modeling clay is a great medium to use for this project, and your students will enjoy personalizing their monsters if you provide other materials that they can easily push into the clay. Your supply of materials could include toothpicks, pipe cleaners, felt scraps, small rhinestones, sequins, shank buttons, small pebbles or aquarium gravel, and pencil-top erasers. When the monsters are completed, have the students name their creatures. Write the name of each monster and the student's name on a folded index card for display.

Four Corners & the Center

Materials: Coins in a cup (a penny, a nickel, a dime, a quarter, and a half-dollar), five hula hoops, five sheets of butcher paper, adhesive tape, broad point marker, CD or tape player and music

Activity: Use this great activity to get the students up, out of their seats, and moving. Cut each piece of butcher paper to the size of the hula hoops by placing a hoop on the paper and tracing around it. Write one number on each circle of butcher paper in large, bold print (1, 5, 10, 25, and 50). Tape the butcher paper onto the hoops. Place one hoop in each corner of the room and one in the center.

Explain to the children that when they hear the music playing, they need to walk around the room. When they hear the music stop, they need to go to the closest hula hoop and stand (or put one foot) inside it. When everyone has found a hoop, draw a coin from the cup. The students standing in the corresponding hoop are "out." Involve the students who are "out" by letting them draw and identify the coins for the subsequent rounds. Continue with the game until only one student is left standing.

Extension: Ask students to determine the "worth" of each hula hoop according to the number of students. For example, if there are four students standing in the dime hula hoop, that station is worth 40 cents. Challenge your students to count off by the value of the coin to determine the total amount for each hoop.

Dear Parents,

We are getting ready to begin our unit on money in math class. Part of our study includes developing an appreciation for money and what it means to earn and save money. To illustrate this concept, we will share a book by Stan and Jan Berenstain called *Trouble with Money*, and we will discuss different ways children can earn and save money.

We will also be creating coin banks in class. Each child will need a small container in which he or she can deposit money. This container could be a small, square tissue box, a potato chip can, a bandage tin, or other container with a removable lid. Small coffee cans will also work, but please make sure there are no sharp edges. The children will be decorating and personalizing their banks, so if you have photographs he or she might want to use, please send those as well. This activity is scheduled for _______________, so please send in a container labeled with your child's name before that date. (Extra containers are appreciated!)

When your child brings the container home, take some time to talk about what he or she learned from our class discussion. If it is possible, you may want to provide opportunities for your child to earn money to deposit into the bank. As always, parental involvement makes a world of difference in a child's academic success!

Thank you for your continued support.

Sincerely,

Math Munchies

Candy Mall

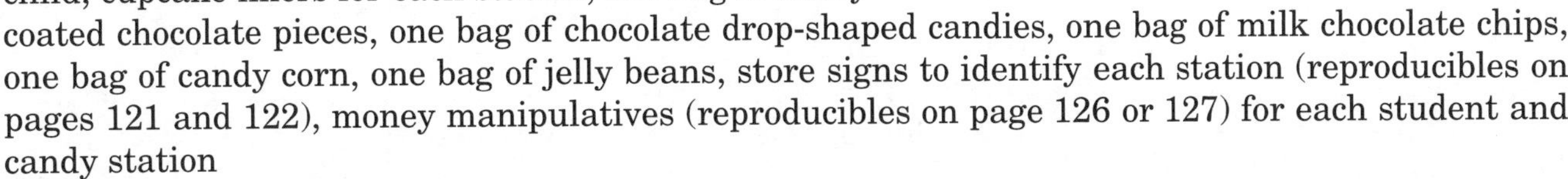

Literature: *Pigs Go to Market: Fun with Math and Shopping*, by Amy Axelrod

Materials: Plastic spoons, one frosted cupcake for each child, cupcake liners for each station, one bag of candy-coated chocolate pieces, one bag of chocolate drop-shaped candies, one bag of milk chocolate chips, one bag of candy corn, one bag of jelly beans, store signs to identify each station (reproducibles on pages 121 and 122), money manipulatives (reproducibles on page 126 or 127) for each student and candy station

Activity: Set up a "candy mall" right in your own classroom and give students everything they need to decorate a sweet snack as well as opportunities to make purchasing decisions, practice making change, and share a fun cooperative learning experience. This is a great activity to do around Halloween, but children will enjoy the story at any time of the year.

First, read the story *Pigs Go to Market: Fun with Math and Shopping*, by Amy Axelrod, to the class. Take time to talk about the story and the decisions the characters made about the products they wanted. Discuss how the decisions might have been different if the characters had only a set amount of money to spend.

Then, begin transforming your classroom into a "candy mall." Set up four or five stations around the room. Use the reproducible store signs to identify the candy shops as well as any others you choose.

You could also select a few students to design their own store signs instead of using the reproducibles. "Hire" storekeepers to begin selling the products and then rotate new storekeepers periodically so that everyone gets a chance to buy and sell. Give each student 20 cents to spend and make sure each station has change. (Empty cupcake liners make great inexpensive containers in which students may put the candies as they buy them.)

Explain that each student will need to go to the cupcake station first to "buy" his cupcake. As students rotate through the stations, buying the decorations they want for their cupcakes, ask them to think about the money they spent and the choices they made. When everyone has finished spending their money and decorating their cupcakes, discuss related vocabulary words and mathematical concepts (e.g., buying, selling, advertising, choice, cost) as the children enjoy their treats.

Counting on Good Behavior

Literature: *Reese's Pieces: Count by Fives*, by Jerry Pallotta

Materials: Chalkboard and chalk or chart paper and marker, three different colors of bingo chips, candy-coated peanut butter candies or other small candies

Activity: Many teachers use bingo chips to reinforce good behavior. This is a great activity to integrate concepts of money and counting into this classroom management tool. Share *Reese's Pieces: Count by Fives*, by Jerry Pallotta, with your students. Draw a nickel and five pennies on the chalkboard. Explain that each nickel is worth five pennies. Give students practice converting pennies to nickels and counting the total amount. For example, draw thirteen pennies on the chalkboard and show students how to convert them to two nickels and three pennies. Then, the students can count "5, 10, 11, 12, 13."

Obtain a generous supply of three different colors of bingo chips. Assign a monetary amount to each color. For example, each pink chip may be worth one penny, each blue chip may be worth one nickel, and each green chip may be worth one dime.

Explain to the students that each student will begin the day with three penny chips. Each time they break a rule, it will cost them one chip. You may choose to give students an opportunity to earn back any chips they have lost. At the end of the day, they can keep the chips they have. The next day, they will receive three more penny chips. At the end of the week, they can "cash in" their penny chips for nickel and dime chips. Then they can use these chips to purchase small items as rewards such as candies, stickers, erasers, or small toys. Determine a realistic price for the items or establish a maximum the students can spend each week so that they will not be able to purchase a large quantity of candy.

Variation: For additional practice in counting coins, provide the students with several copies of the reproducible on page 126. Give each child a certain amount of "nickels" to cut out. Then, have the students count the coins by fives and also exchange their nickels with the equivalent amount of money in quarters. You may wish to distribute candy treats when students have mastered this skill.

Jelly Bean Bin

2 for 5¢

or

3¢ each

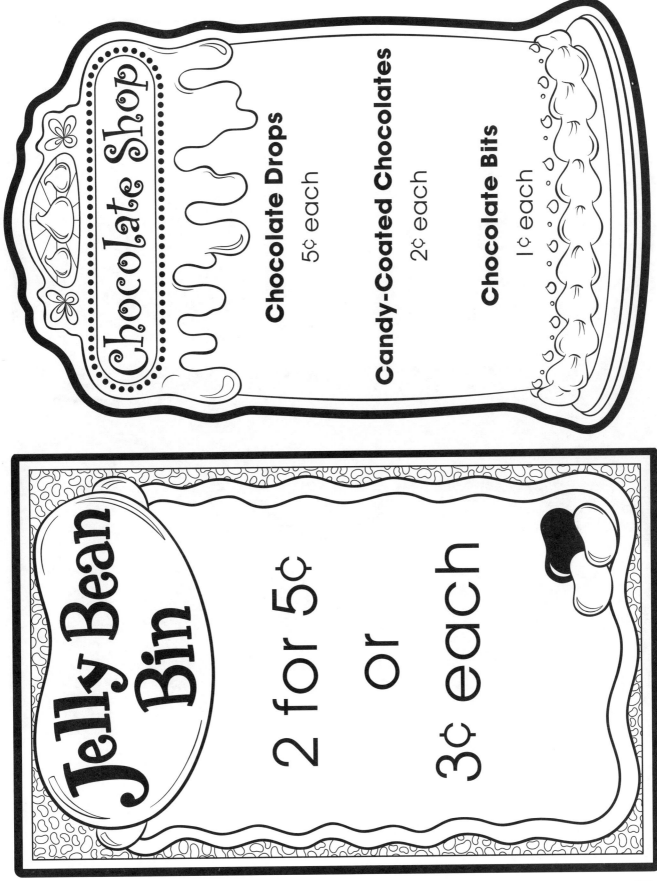

Chocolate Shop

Chocolate Drops

5¢ each

Candy-Coated Chocolates

2¢ each

Chocolate Bits

1¢ each

The Bakery
Cupcakes
6¢ each
Candy Corner
Candy Corn
2¢ each

Easy Come, Easy Go

Literature: *Alexander Who Used to Be Rich Last Sunday*, by Judith Viorst

Materials: Backpack or large plastic resealable storage bag, a copy of *Alexander Who Used to be Rich Last Sunday*, an envelope of paper money manipulatives (1 dollar bill or coin, 10 pennies, 7 dimes, and 4 nickels made from the reproducible page 126 or 127), a copy of the reproducible parent letter on page 124, response sheet on page 125

Activity: This simple activity is a good way to provide an opportunity for parents and children to spend a few minutes reading and responding to literature together as well as reinforcing the concepts of spending money and making change. Prepare a take-home pack by placing the following items in a large resealable plastic bag or backpack: a copy of the book, an envelope of paper money manipulatives from page 126 or 127, a copy of the parent letter from page 124, and a copy of the response sheet from page 125.

Explain to the students that they will take turns taking the pack home to share with their parents. As they read the book with their parents, the students will "spend" their play money just as Alexander does in the story. When they have finished reading the book, they will respond to the story by completing the "A Penny for Your Thoughts" response sheet (copy of page 125).

When each student returns the pack to school, remove the response sheets and display them in the room on a bulletin board where the students can read them. Students will enjoy sharing with their peers the responses they wrote with their parents' help, and parents should enjoy this opportunity to read with their children.

Variation: This activity could also be prepared using the book, *Jelly Beans for Sale*, by Bruce McMillan. McMillan uses photographs to illustrate coin equivalencies to purchase jelly beans. As the children purchase jelly beans, the author shows several different ways to reach each monetary value. Revise the parent letter and draw a jelly bean shape at the bottom of the page for the readers' response. Assemble a take-home pack similar to the one described above, with the book, an envelope of paper money, the parent letter, and a small treat of jelly beans that the students can enjoy with their parents when they have finished the activity.

A $100 Day

Materials: Parent letter from page 128, $100 in paper play money, journal or notebook and pencil

Activity: Provide each student with a copy of the parent letter on page 128. Explain to students that you are "giving them" $100 to spend any way they want. Remind them to share their thoughts about what they would like to buy with their parents and then use newspaper advertisements or catalogs to verify pricing. Together, the students can work with their parents to record their thoughts in a journal. Younger children may need more assistance writing the entry, whereas older children may be able to complete this task independently. Have a copy of a book list of money-related literature available for those parents who request it.

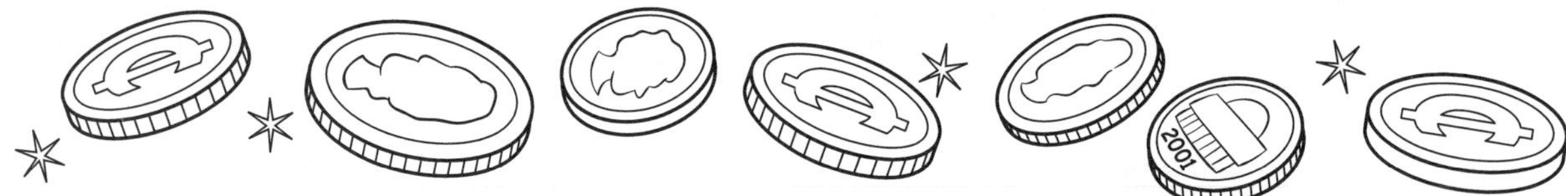

Dear Parents,

We are currently studying money is math class. We are working hard to recognize coins and understand the concepts of spending, saving, and making change. In this pack, you will find the book, *Alexander Who Used to be Rich Last Sunday*, by Judith Viorst, and an envelope of paper money. Please take a few minutes to sit with your child and enjoy this story about a young boy who realizes how easy it is to spend money. As you read the story, give your child an opportunity to spend his or her play money just like Alexander does. At the end of the story, your child should have the same amount of money left as the character in the story.

When you have finished, take a moment to cut out the penny pattern on the enclosed sheet. On the back of the penny, help your child write a sentence or two to respond to this book. Here are some ideas to get you started:

- My favorite part of the book is . . .
- I like this book because . . .
- If I were Alexander, I would have . . .

Remind your child to write his or her name on the penny. Then, place the book, paper money, and penny pattern back in the bag. Return everything to school by ______________________________ so another family can enjoy this at-home activity. The next time you visit our classroom, please look at our "Penny for Your Thoughts" display to see what others thought of this book.

Thank you for your continued support and assistance.

Sincerely,

A Penny for Your Thoughts

Easy Come, Easy Go

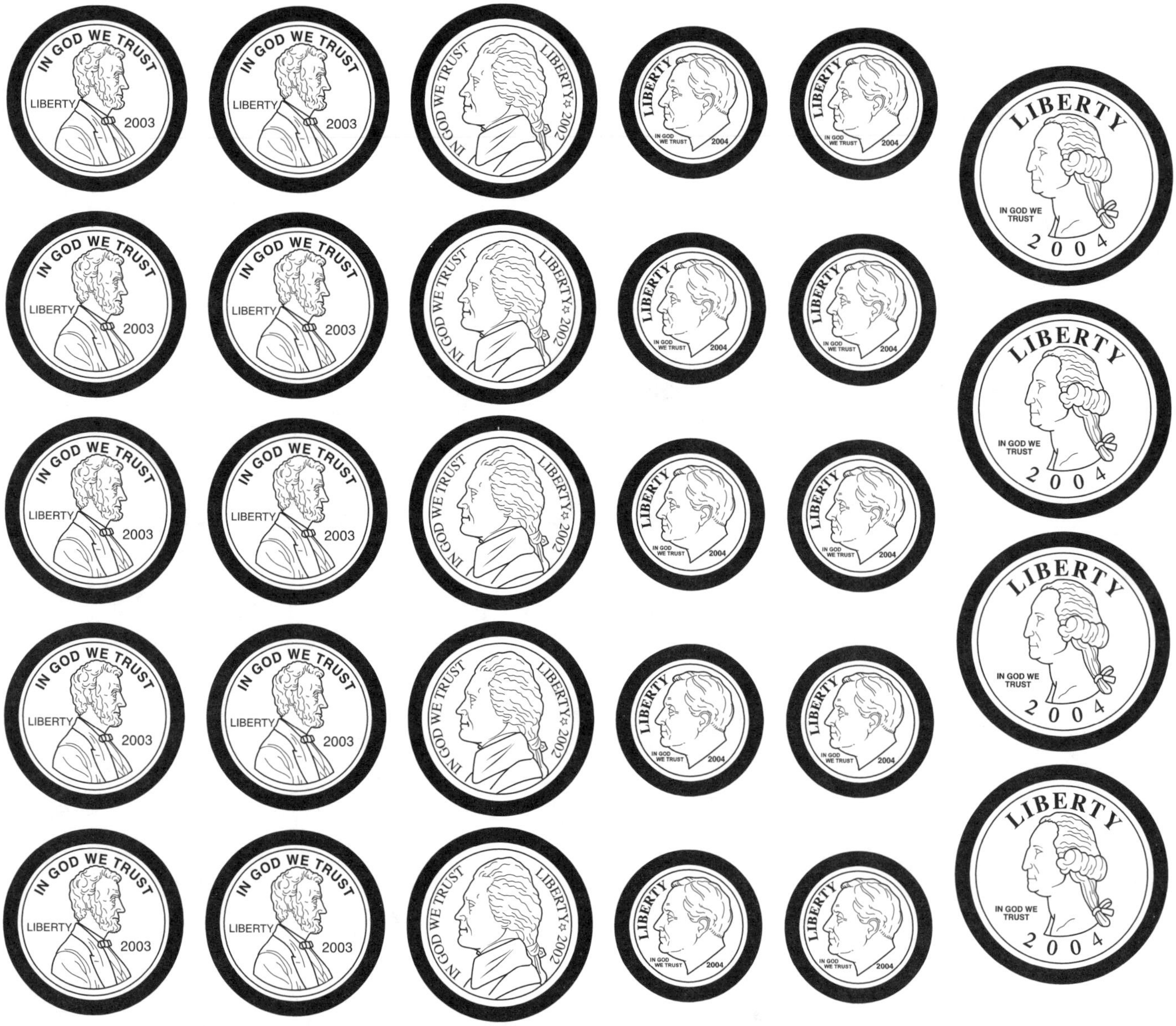

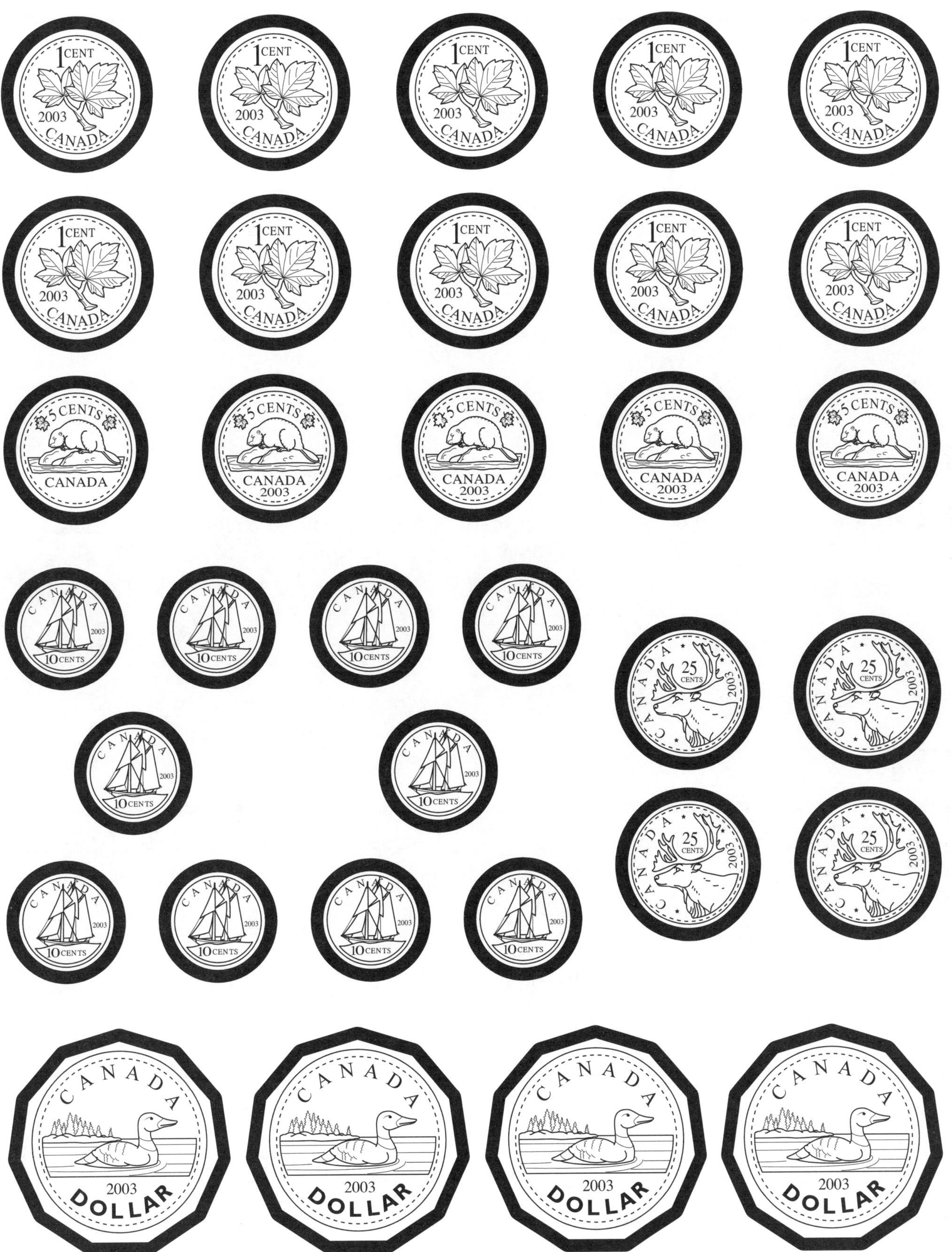
1 CENT
2003
CANADA
5 CENTS
CANADA
2003
10 CENTS
25 CENTS
DOLLAR

Dear Parents,

We are studying money in class and your child is about to have a hundred-dollar day! You can help by talking with your child about how he or she would spend $100. Reinforce the concept of money sense by making sure that he or she has selected realistic items. Use catalogs, advertisements from newspapers, and realistic monetary amounts of the desired items as you discuss what your child would like to buy. Help your child, if necessary, to write his or her thoughts in a journal or notebook. Encourage your child to be creative! Cut out the $100 bill on the bottom of this form, and use the back to record the shopping list.

There are many great money-related literature books that you may wish to read with your child. *Monster Money*, by Loreen Leedy, and *Arthur's Funny Money*, by Lillian Hoban, are two enjoyable books that will help children understand the concept of earning and spending money. Spending time reading with your child in the evening is a wonderful way to end the day. If you would like a copy of the entire money-related book list for your next trip to the public library, please let me know. I will be happy to provide it for you. As always, thank you for your priceless help!

Sincerely,